crochet jewelry

crochet jewelry

By Sophie Britten

The Taunton Press
Inspiration for hands-on living®

The Taunton Press
63 South Main Street
PO Box 5506
Newtown, CT 06470-5506
www.taunton.com

The publishers have made every effort to ensure
that all instructions given in this book are
accurate and safe but they cannot accept liability
for any resulting injury, damage, or loss to either
person or property, whether direct or
consequential and howsoever arising. The
author and publishers will be grateful for any
information which will assist them in keeping
future editions up to date

ISBN-10 1-56158-944-6
ISBN-13 978-1-56158-944-9

Library of Congress Cataloging-in-Publication data

Britten, Sophie.
  Crochet jewelry / by Sophie Britten.
      p. cm.
  Includes bibliographical references and index.
  ISBN-13: 978-1-56158-944-9 (alk. paper)
  ISBN-10: 1-56158-944-6 (alk. paper)
  1. Jewelry making. 2. Crocheting. I. Title.
  TT212.B75 2007
  745.594'2--dc22
                                2006018591

Set in Syntax LT

Printed and bound in China by Toppan
Printing Company Ltd

Senior Executive Editor Anna Sanderson
Executive Art Editor Rhonda Summerbell
Editor Sue Whiting
Proofreader Naomi Waters
Photography Roger Dixon
Design Colin Goody
Production Faizah Malik

Sophie Britten

crochet jewelry

35 fantastic pieces of jewelry to make & wear

The Taunton Press

Contents

introduction

Crochet, knitting, and other home crafts have never been more popular and crochet jewelry is the latest cool craft that will have you reaching for your hook and making amazing things in no time at all.

Crochet is a wonderful and versatile craft that has been entertaining fingers for centuries. It has evolved over time from beautiful and intricate lace-making to a craft that rivals knitting for its suitability for making clothes and now to a unique way of making jewelry.

Crochet Jewelry is packed full of over 35 original and exciting ideas for all different styles of jewelry at all different levels. Whether you're going for boho chic, high glamour, or sexy sophistication, there are ideas here for every occasion!

As the basis for crochet is a series of chain stitches, it is the ideal medium for making jewelry and perfect for creating necklaces or bracelets; you can even use jewelry wire for a really unusual look. Crochet is also a great way of making flowers and other motifs that can be used as pendants, brooches, or on hair clips. There are dozens of different methods using a wide variety of materials, such as conventional wools, sparkly yarns, wire, beads, ribbons, bangles, hair clips, and even curtain rings.

The book includes a fully illustrated how-to section, which will give you all the basics of crochet and jewelry-making, plus useful information on all the materials you might need, and loads of helpful tips.

All the patterns are skill-rated and include easy-to-follow instructions. Most patterns are easy enough for a beginner, with some more challenging and intricate pieces for the more experienced crocheter. However, most of the patterns are ingeniously straightforward and many projects can be completed in a couple of hours or less. So for unique hand-made jewelry with a difference, *Crochet Jewelry* is the perfect book for you. I hope you enjoy making the projects!

materials

Crochet is amazingly versatile. You can use any kind of wire, yarn, string – even strips of fabric – and you can also work in conjunction with a wide variety of other materials, such as rings, bangles, beads, shells, sequins, in fact, anything that can be crocheted into, or that can be threaded onto the yarn. This book concentrates on wire and yarn and materials that are most suitable for jewelry-making. Here is a comprehensive list of all the materials that you might need to make the projects in this book. More detailed descriptions of jewelry findings and tools are found on pages 25–7.

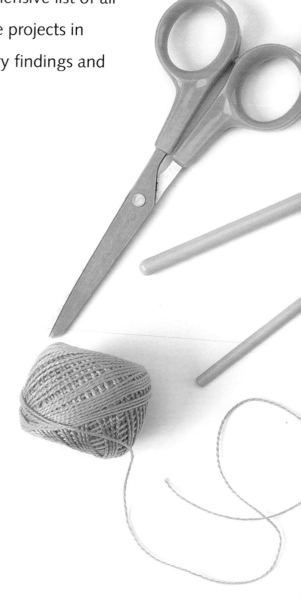

Crochet hooks: Hook sizes used in this book vary from A (2mm) to K (6.5mm). For tips on choosing the right hook, and a full hook conversion chart, go to page 10.

Tapestry needles: Large blunt needles that won't split the yarn are used for sewing in ends.

Sewing needles: It is useful to have a collection of different-sized needles on hand as these projects use varying thicknesses of thread and yarn.

Tape measure: useful for measuring size and gauge.

Small sharp scissors: for cutting yarn and fine wire.

Jewelry findings: including clasps, pin backs, earring hooks. These are available in silver or gold plate and in varying shapes and sizes.

Crimps: These are small metal rings that, when crushed flat, firmly grip a piece of yarn and will therefore hold a bead or clasp in place.

Jump rings: small rings used for joining. These are very useful for making earrings or necklaces and can be used to join the work to an earring hook or clasp.

Pliers: Both round-nosed and flat-nosed pliers are very useful jewelry-making pieces of equipment.

For full instructions on how to use these, go to the jewelry-making section.

Wire cutters: Fine wire can easily be cut with a pair of scissors. However for thicker wire, more than 0.6mm, you will need a pair of wire cutters.

Beads: Beads feature very prominently in the book and are widely available in millions of gorgeous hues in all different shapes and sizes. Bead recommendations are given for each pattern. However, if you cannot source these exact beads, the main thing to check is that the hole is big enough to accommodate the yarn you are using.

Beading needles: There are various types of needles used for threading beads. For a full explanation, go to the jewelry-making section.

Jewelry wire: Crocheting with wire is very versatile: it can be worked in simple chains or used to create a fine mesh fabric. It creates a wonderfully unusual and irregular fabric. Take care when working with wire as it cannot be undone as easily as yarn and over-stressing the wire by pulling out stitches may weaken it. More information on wire gauge is found on page 30.

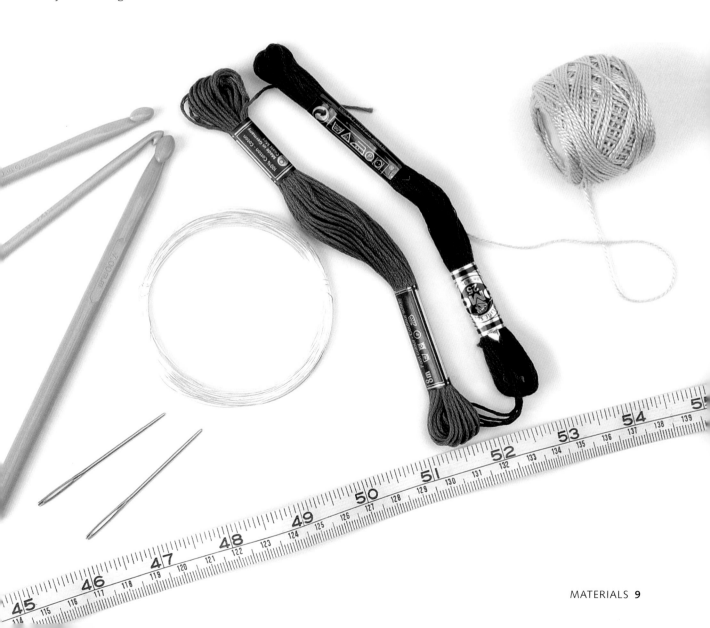

Thick jewelry wire: 0.6mm andmm wire are used in this book to add hold, shape or texture; 0.4mm wire is used to create pendant beads.

Yarn: Recent years have seen an explosion of fabulous multicolored, textured, spangly, and chunky yarns and there is now a dazzling array to choose from. This book mainly uses fine yarns such as sparkly Goldfingering and lightweight cottons that are perfect for making small pieces such as jewelry.

Glue: indispensable for attaching pin backs, and other minor jobs. Use a strong glue such as an epoxy or superglue.

Crochet hook conversion chart

Regular crochet hooks vary in size from A (2mm) to S (19mm) and are 6in (15cm) long. They are available in plastic and aluminum and wood, with the larger hooks being in lightweight plastic. Steel hooks, which are sized differently than regular crochet hooks, are much smaller and are used for intricate lace making and filet work.

This book uses metric sizes for the hooks, but you may find that different pattern books use different systems to express the sizes. This chart will help you to choose the right hook. If you find your work is too tight, use a larger hook. Similarly, if it is too loose, you may need to use a smaller hook.

METRIC (mm)	US	UK & CANADIAN
2.00	A	14
2.25	B/1	13
2.50	-	12
2.75	C/2	-
3.00	-	11
3.25	D/3	10
3.50	E/4	9
3.75	F/5	-
4.00	G/6	8
4.50	-	7
5.00	H/8	6
5.50	I/9	5
6.00	J/10	4
6.50	K/10½	3
7.00	-	2
8.00	L/11	0
9.00	M/13	00
10.00	N/15	000
15.0	P/19	
16.0	Q	
19.0	S/35	

learning to crochet

Crochet is a fantastic craft and a great creative outlet. It is also an ingenious way of making jewelry. Even the most basic techniques that you will learn over these pages can be used to create stunning and professional-looking jewelry. The great thing about crochet is that, unlike knitting, you work one complete stitch at a time and so avoid the risk of dropping a stitch. This is especially useful when working with fine, and otherwise hard to see, materials.

The basics of crochet are very simple and once you have mastered the basic action of the hook in one hand, and the control of the yarn in the other, you will be able to make beautiful things in no time.

When you first start off, it is important that you can see what you are doing, and learn to recognize the stitches and their composition. So for practical purposes start with a smooth, thick yarn such as a dk (double knitting) or 4-ply in a pale color and a G (4mm) crochet hook.

HOLDING THE HOOK – RIGHT HANDED
Hold the flat part of the hook between the thumb and index finger of your right hand. There are two ways of holding the hook: either like a knife with the end of the hook in the palm of your hand, or like a pen, with the end of your hook over your hand. You should use whichever method you find most comfortable [see below].

HOLDING THE YARN – RIGHT HANDED

The yarn is controlled by your left hand. To control the feed, wrap the yarn from the ball around your little finger, under the third and middle fingers, and over your index finger (so the tail end hangs over your palm). Extend the index finger to control the yarn and hold the work firmly between the thumb and middle finger. There should be a space of about 2in (5cm) between the work and your extended finger [see below].

INSTRUCTIONS FOR LEFTIES

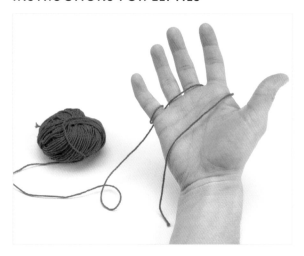

The instructions for crocheting with the left hand are exactly the same as those for the right, except the position of the hook and the yarn is reversed, so lefties should hold the hook in their left hand and the yarn in their right and reverse the instructions [see above and below]. It may be helpful to prop the book in front of a mirror.

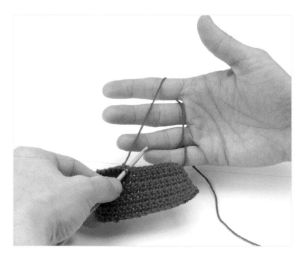

SLIP KNOT

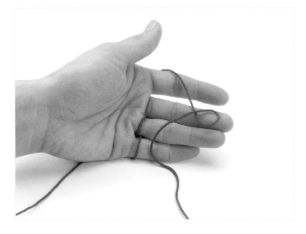

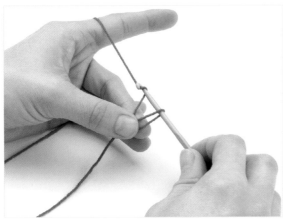

In almost all cases, crochet starts with a slip knot. Leaving a tail of around 6in (15cm) (the pattern may say if you should leave more or less), make a loop [see top picture, above]. Now insert the hook into the loop from front to back and draw another loop through it. [see lower picture, above]. Pull the knot close to the hook, but not too tight.

CHAIN STITCH (CH)

The first row of crochet is made by working a series of chain stitches (ch). This row is known as the base chain or foundation row.

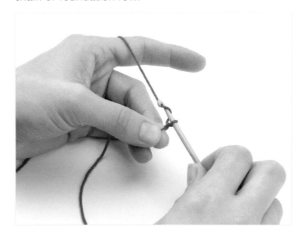

To make a chain, hold the slip knot between the thumb and middle finger of your left hand, keeping the yarn taut, push the hook forward and under the yarn, then over the yarn in a circular motion (this is called yarn over, or yo) [see above].

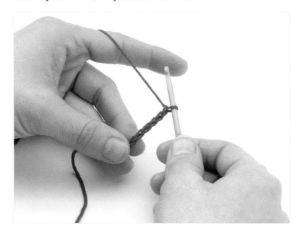

Now draw the yarn through the loop on the hook [see above]. This makes one chain stitch. Take care not to make your work too tight. Each stitch must be large enough for you to be able to fit the hook comfortably into it.

As you make more chains, maintain the gauge by keeping a firm grip on your work; this will mean moving the thumb and middle finger of your left hand along the work so that your grip remains close to the hook.

If you are completely new to crochet, practice making chains until you have a smooth action and can easily make even chains of the same size. This is a good way of getting used to the feel of the hook and the yarn.

Once you have mastered this very simple and basic crochet technique, you are ready to make a surprising range of beautiful and classically elegant jewelry. These chain necklaces are very quick to make and even a complete beginner can achieve fantastic results.

Above: This necklace uses a fine yarn threaded with azure glass beads worked in evenly spaced clusters along a strand of chain stitches.

Above: This necklace is composed of fine silver jewelry wire and amethyst chips worked in strands of crochet chains. This shows how the crochet chains create a unique take on a conventional jewelry chain. The wonderful thing about crochet is how easily beads or gems can be incorporated into the work.

These two projects give you an idea of the diverse effects this very simply technique can have and its ideal suitability to jewelry-making

basic stitches

These are the first and most basic stitches that you will use in crochet. They are also the most useful and a basis for many variations. These stitches all use the same basic technique, the key difference being their heights. You will often use these stitches in combination with one another, as working with different height stitches allows you to create all kinds of wonderful shapes and patterns and is an essential tool for making motifs such as flowers.

SINGLE CROCHET (SC)

This is the simplest and most common fabric-making stitch. This is a very easy stitch to make and will soon seem like second nature to you. As the simplest stitch, it is ideal for making wire mesh as it doesn't overwork the wire. When worked with yarn it creates a compact fabric.

Insert the hook into the next stitch from front to back [see above] (or second chain from the hook if you are starting from the base chain), yarn over,

draw the hook towards you through the fabric, yarn over and draw the hook through both loops on the hook [see above]. You are left with one loop on the hook. This is one single crochet. Repeat into the next stitch or chain. Work until the very last stitch or chain. This is one row of single crochet.

At the end of the row, turn the work, now make one chain stitch – this is your turning chain – and work one sc into each stitch of the previous row, making sure to insert the hook under both loops of the stitch you are crocheting into.

HALF DOUBLE (HDC)

This stitch is slightly taller than single crochet. Wrap the yarn around the hook before inserting the hook into the next stitch [see above] (or third chain from the hook), yarn over, draw the hook through the work, yarn over, draw the hook through all three loops on the hook [see below], leaving just one loop on the hook. This is one half double crochet.

When you reach the end of the row, turn the work, make two chains and continue, working the first hdc into the top of the last stitch of the previous row. Continue to work one hdc into each stitch of the previous row, omitting the turning chain at the end.

DOUBLE CROCHET (DC)

This stitch is taller yet. As with hdc, start by wrapping the yarn around the hook and insert the hook into the next stitch (or fourth chain from the hook), yarn over, draw the hook through the work, yarn over, draw the hook through the first two loops on the hook, yarn over [see above], draw the hook through the remaining two loops on the hook [see below], leaving just one loop on the hook. This is one double crochet.

When you reach the end of the row, turn the work, make three chains; these count as the first stitch of the next row. Skip the first dc (last dc of the previous row) and insert the hook into the second stitch of the new row. Continue to work until the end of the row, inserting the last dc into the top of the turning chain of the row below.

TRIPLE CROCHET (TR)

This is taller than double crochet and creates a less dense fabric. Wrap the yarn over twice [see above], insert hook into the next stitch (or fifth chain from the hook), yarn over, draw the hook through the work, *yarn over, draw the hook through two loops; repeat from * twice more until one loop remains on the hook [see below].

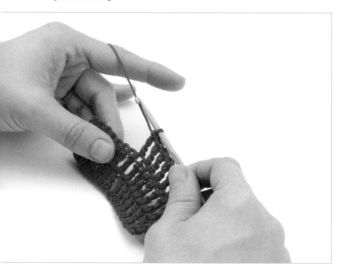

DOUBLE TREBLE (DTR)

Even taller than the triple crochet stitch, this is made by wrapping the yarn around the hook three times before inserting it into the next stitch (or sixth chain from hook), yarn over, draw the hook through the work, *yarn over, draw the hook through two loops; repeat from * thre more times until one loop remains on the hook [see above].

SLIP STITCH (SL ST)

This is the shortest stitch and is mostly used for joining or shaping. Insert the hook into a stitch or chain (always remember to insert the hook under both strands of the stitch), yarn over; draw the hook through the fabric and the loop on the hook [see above]. You are left with just one loop on the hook. This is one slip stitch.

making fabric

Crochet fabric starts with a base chain, which is a series of chain stitches and is worked in any given stitch from right to left in rows.

The two keys things to know when making fabric are where to place the first stitch of the first row, and how many turning chains a particular stitch requires. These tables indicate the requirements for each stitch.

FIRST ROW

Single crochet Insert hook into 2nd ch from hook.
Half double crochet Insert hook into 3rd ch from hook.
Double crochet Insert hook into 4th ch from hook.
Triple crochet Insert hook into 5th ch from hook.
Double triple crochet Insert hook into 6th ch from hook.

TURNING CHAINS

The number of chains you make at the beginning of a row depends on the height of the stitch and, except when working in single crochet or half double crochet (or where the pattern says otherwise), replaces the first stitch of the new row. Remember: Always turn the work in the same direction to avoid twisting your stitches.

Single crochet: 1ch, insert hook into first stitch of new row.

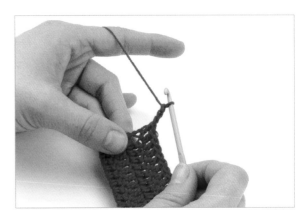

Half double crochet: 2ch, insert hook into first stitch of new row.

Double crochet: 3ch, insert hook into second stitch of new row.

Triple crochet: 4ch, insert hook into second stitch of new row.

Double triple crochet: 5ch, insert hook into second stitch of new row.

BASIC RULES

After each stitch has been completed there should be just one loop on the hook.

Always insert the hook into the stitch from front to back unless you are instructed otherwise.

Always insert the hook under the top two loops of the chain or stitch, unless the stitch or pattern says otherwise.

When counting chains, do not include the loop on the hook, e.g., if the pattern requires 25 chain stitches, you should have 25 plus the one on the hook.

working in the round

As an alternative to working from right to left, crochet can also be worked in rounds. This is a very useful technique that is used in many of the patterns in this book. It is used to create a basic circle, as a base for flower motifs, to make 3-D projects such as balls and tubes, and is also an essential technique when making hats, bags, and other rounded items.

When working in the round, the equivalent to the base chain is a ring. As with flat fabric, start by making a slip knot. To make the ring, make a series of chains and join the last chain to the first with a slip stitch. To make the first round, work 1ch, then work as many stitches as you need into the center of the ring and complete the round with a sl st into the first ch.

To make a flat disc of concentric rounds, increase by the original number of stitches in each round.
e.g.: Make 5ch, join in a ring with a sl st.
1st Round 1ch, work 10sc into ring, sl st into first sc.
2nd Round 1ch, 2sc into each sc to end, sl st into first sc. (20 sts)
3rd Round 1ch, *1sc into next sc, 2sc into next sc; repeat from * to end, sl st into first sc. (30 sts)
Continue in this way, working an extra 10sc in each round.

Spiral shaping is a quick variation on concentric rounds, but instead of starting and closing each round, each round is a continuation of the last [see above]. You may need to use a marker or a different colored piece of yarn to show where the round starts and finishes.

Another great use of the round is to make tubes. Make a ring as before, work as many stitches as you need around it (either into the ring or into each ch), and continue to work in a spiral without increasing or decreasing.

tip
Always finish the row or round you are working on when you put your work down to avoid losing your place in the pattern.

gauge

This is the number of rows and stitches per inch (centimetre), usually measured over a square of fabric. The gauge will determine the size of the finished project. This is obviously of vital importance when making clothes, and less so when making non-fitting items such as jewelry. The most important thing is that your gauge is consistent – this will make a nice even fabric. And in the case of earrings, or other items made in pairs, it will ensure that they are both the same size.

When working with wire, the gauge can be difficult to control, but this is part of the charm of the medium and an uneven fabric can look more attractive.

To keep your gauge even, it is a good idea to practice on a piece of scrap crochet to warm up each time you start a project, and in particular if you are going back to a half-completed project.

When using yarn to make bigger pieces of crochet, you need to make a gauge swatch to measure your gauge. Crochet a square of fabric in the stitch pattern given, making the square at least 4in (10cm) in both directions [see above, left and right]. Measure out the distance stated in the gauge and count how many stitches there are within this measurement. If there are too few, your crochet is loose and you need to start again using a smaller size hook. If there are too many stitches, your crochet is tight and you ned to try again using a larger size hook.

basic techniques

There are an infinite number of variations on the basic stitches that can be used to create all kinds of wonderful shapes and textures. As with knitting, fabric is most often shaped by increasing or decreasing the number of stitches in a row or round. Here are a few basic techniques for shaping and mastering crochet.

INCREASING

DECREASING

To decrease, two or more stitches are worked together. To decrease one stitch in single crochet (**sc2tog**), insert hook into the next st, yarn over, draw loop through the work (two loops on the hook), insert hook into the next st, yo, draw loop through the work, yo, draw hook through all three loops [see above], leaving just one loop.

To increase, simply work one or more extra stitches into the next stitch. A single increase is made by working two stitches into the same stitch. You can, of course, increase by more than one stitch at a time.

work two double crochet stitches together as follows: *yarn over, insert hook into next st, yo, draw through a loop, yo, draw hook through two of the loops on the hook (leaving two loops); repeat this step from * once more, leaving three loops on the hook, yo, draw the

To decrease by two stitches in single crochet (**sc3tog**), work three stitches together as follows: insert hook into next st, yarn over, draw loop through the work, insert hook into next st, yo, draw loop through the work, insert hook into next st, yo, draw the hook though the work, yrh and draw the loop through all four loops, leaving just one loop [see above].

To decrease one stitch in double crochet (**dc2tog**),

hook through all three loops on the hook [see below]. The principle of decreasing is to work the stitch as normal until only two loops remain on the hook, insert the hook into the next stitch, work the stitch as normal until there are only three loops on the hook; and so on. To complete the decrease: yo and draw the

ADDING NEW YARN AND CHANGING COLOR

None of the patterns requires more than one ball of yarn; however you may need to add a new color. The technique is the same. Change yarns during the last stitch in the row or round by working the last loop of the stitch using the new yarn before you need to change yarn, so the new color is ready to be used for the turning chain or next stitch.

finishing

It is very important to take time and care when finishing a project even if you are tempted to rush the final stages. The projects in this book require many different types of finishing, but they all have one thing in common – they will all have ends that need to be sewn in. It is worth doing it right as otherwise you may have an unsightly (and uncomfortable) spike of wire projecting from your necklace, or a stray strand poking through a hair clip.

FASTENING OFF

Cut the yarn, leaving roughly 4in (10cm) (if you are going to use the tail to attach a popper or hook, it should be a bit longer). Make 1 chain, draw the tail through the chain, and pull firmly [see above]. Weave in the end 1in (2.5cm) in one direction and then back the other way for a neat and secure finish. Cut off the excess yarn.

You do not need a needle to weave in wire ends as you can weave the wire directly into the fabric, but take care not to distort the shape of the jewelry.

If you are working with yarn, use a blunt-tipped tapestry needle that won't split it.

BLOCKING

Occasionally the pattern will instruct you to press the finished item. Place the item under a piece of damp cloth and iron flat. The Goldfingering items will benefit particularly from pressing.

CARE OF FINISHED ITEMS

Wire projects should be handled gently as excessive bending could weaken the wire, which may then eventually break.

Yarn projects should be fairly robust and may be washed. Care instructions for particular yarns should be given on the yarn label; however, where there are none or you are unsure, you should wash a sample piece first.

following instructions

Crochet patterns use special terms that are often abbreviated or shown as symbols on a chart in order to make the pattern easier to follow. Before you start a project, make sure you understand the instructions and are familiar with all the terms and techniques. A few of the patterns here offer different sizes. To make the pattern easier to follow, go through the pattern before you start, clearly marking which size you are going to make and highlighting all instructions for that size throughout the pattern.

ABBREVIATIONS

This is a list of the most common abbreviations and all those that are used in this book, but is not an exhaustive list as there are many different crochet stitches, not all of which are used here.

beg	beginning	**in**	inches	**tch**	turning chain
blo	back loop only	**inc**	increase	**tog**	together
ch	chain	**patt**	pattern	**tr**	triple crochet
ch sp	chain space	**rem**	remaining	**WS**	wrong side
cm	centimeters	**rep**	repeat	**yo**	yarn over
cont	continue	**RS**	right side	*****	Where there is a recurring instruction, the section to be repeated is marked with an asterisk, e.g.: *3dc into next ch sp, 1sc into next sc, 3dc into next ch sp; repeat pattern from * until last st.
dc	double crochet	**sc**	single crochet		
dch	double chain	**scb**	single crochet with a bead		
dec	decrease				
dtr	double treble	**sp**	space		Peter Have inserted 'single crochet' entry and changed 'ss' to 'sl st' to match earlier text.
flo	front loop only	**sl st**	slip stitch		
foll	following	**st(s)**	stitch(es)		

jewelry-making techniques

The projects in this book use simple jewelry-making techniques that can be easily incorporated into crocheted works. In addition to the usual crochet materials, such as hooks and needles, you will also need some of the essential jewelry-making tools.

In conventional jewelry-making, there are a huge array of tools and equipment and hundreds of different types of findings available in a wide variety of materials. To keep things simple, only a few key tools are used in these projects. In case you are not already familiar with them, here are some notes on which materials you might need and how they are to be used.

Findings: This is a generic term that includes a vast array of jewelry-making accessories, such as clasps, earring backs and hooks, pin backs, rings, and jump rings, as well as many other items not used in this book, such as bead tips, spacers, head pins, and so on.

tip

If you don't have a beading needle, or it has disappeared into the carpet, here's a handy tip for threading beads onto yarn or thread.

Cut a piece of wire 3in (7.5cm) or so long. Fold it over the yarn near the end. Twist one end of the wire a couple of turns very tightly around the other and lay this first end alongside the yarn. Now use the tip of the wire like a needle [see below].

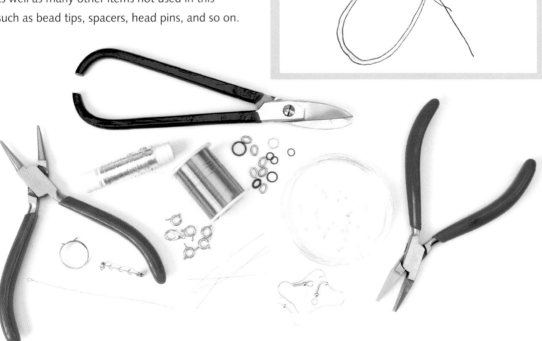

Round-nosed pliers: Pliers are absolutely indispensable in jewelry-making for taking the fuss out of fiddly jobs. Round-nosed pliers are used for bending wire into a loop [see above].

Crimps: very small metal rings used to finish off a strand of beads. The cord goes through the crimp, through the clasp, and back through the crimp, which is then flattened with a pair of flat-nosed pliers to secure the cord [see above]. These are not to be used with wire as the wire will snap when the crimp is crushed.

Head pins: These straight pins come in varying lengths and are characterized by having a flattened end – this allows you to thread beads onto the pin without them falling off. The beaded pins can be incorporated into all types of jewelry by making a loop at the tail end.

Jump rings: plain wire rings of any size, usually round or oval in shape, used for attaching jewelry parts. These are generally not soldered closed, but can be opened and closed by pushing the ends together. When using them with fine wire, seal with a dab of glue on the join.

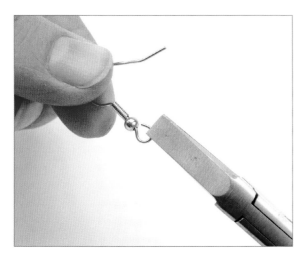

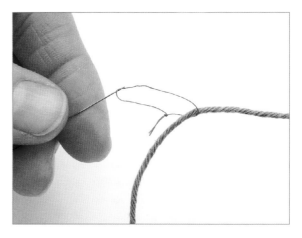

Flat-nosed pliers: These are very handy tools that you will use all the time for crushing crimps, opening and closing rings on necklaces, earrings, and other items of jewelry [see above].

Rigid beading needles: These are needles in the conventional sense, but they are very slim and the eye is very narrow – too narrow, in fact, for conventional beading thread, let alone yarn. Make a leader by threading a short length of fine thread through the eye and tying it to create a loop; you can now pass your yarn through this much more ample loop [see above].

Wire cutters: a sturdy cutting tool for medium to thick wire. Fine gauge wire can be easily cut using a pair of regular scissors.

Collapsible eye beading needle: a piece of fine grade steel wire twisted around itself, leaving a loop at the top to make an eye. The loop is flexible and is, as its name suggests, collapsible, so that the needle can be pulled through even the smallest bead hole.

beading

There are all sorts of wonderful instruments for beading, such as spinners that allow you to thread beads very quickly and layout boards for designing complicated bead arrangements. However, the beading in these patterns is kept fairly simple. Here are a few easy principles to assist you.

When crocheting with beads, you should thread all the beads you will need for the project onto the yarn or wire (still attached to the ball or reel) before you start to crochet. With large quantities of beads, it is a good idea to add a few more than you think you will need in case you have miscounted. These can be discarded at the end.

Thread the beads in the reverse order to the one in which they will be needed (i.e., the beads you need first are threaded last and vice versa).

Always work in good light. Frustration and strained eyes will result from working without proper lighting.

Work on a light-colored towel or fabric surface. This will stop the beads from bouncing all over the place when you drop them and you can easily retrieve all the dropped beads at the end.

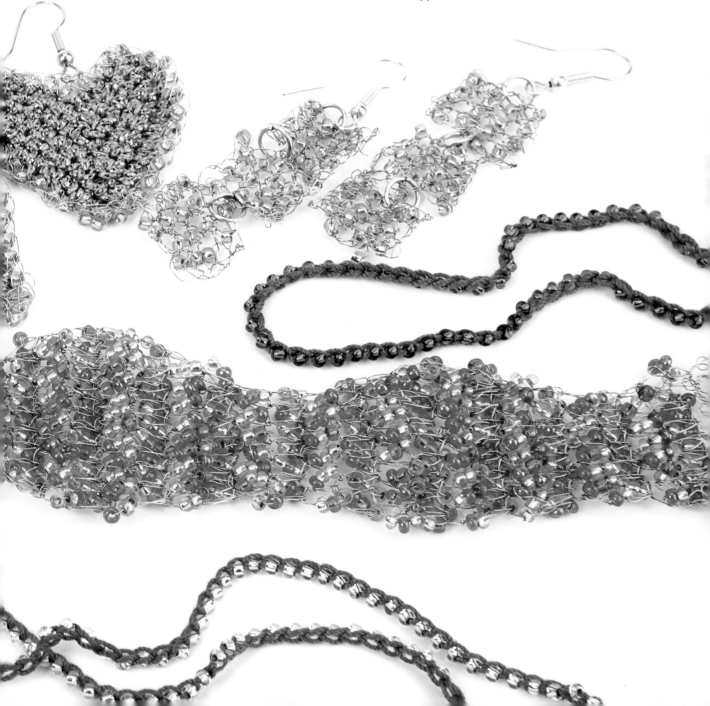

wire

Jewelry wire comes in various gauges and is generally available in silver, copper, and gold colors. You can crochet with any fine wire. In fact the finer the wire, the more flexible it will be and the more fluid your work; conversely, thicker wire may be too stiff and difficult to work with. The wire chart below will help you choose the correct wire. A good tip if you are planning to make a lot of wire projects is to use fuse wire, which can be bought fairly cheaply for a large reel.

WIRE DIAMETER CONVERSION CHART

Gauge	mm	Inches
32	0.2	0.008
30	0.25	0.010
28	0.32	0.012
26	.4	0.015
24	.5	0.020
22	.6	0.025
20	.8	0.03
18	1.0	0.04
16	1.2	0.05
15	1.45	0.0571
14	1.63	0.0641

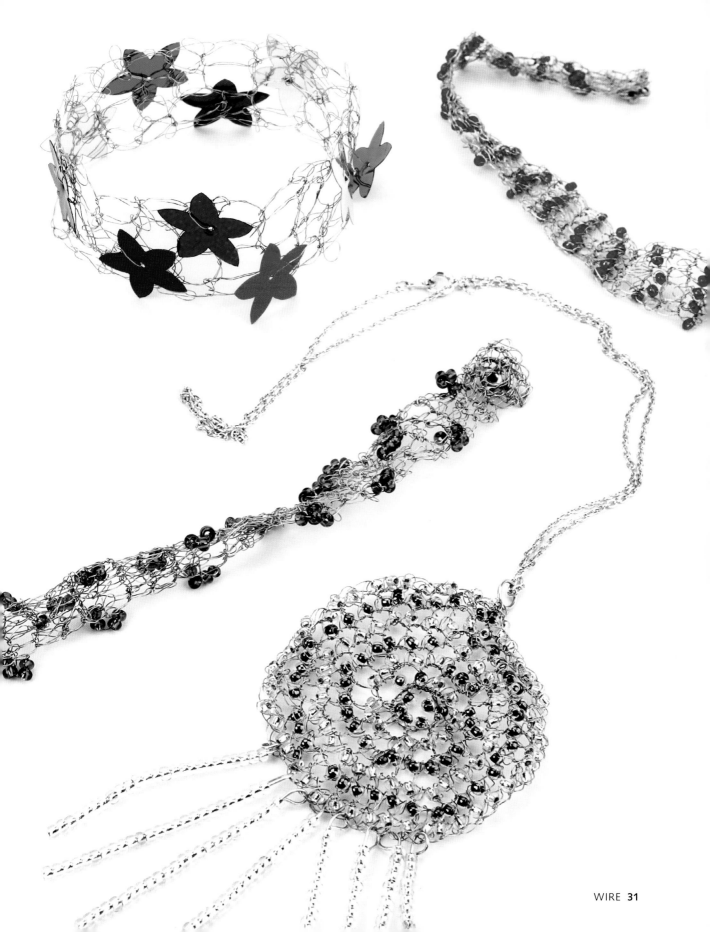

what you can make

amethyst and bead necklace

Using just chain stitches interspersed with beads and amethyst chips, you will be surprised at how quick and easy this necklace is to make. Composed of five beaded strands attached to a clasp at each end, this is a really pretty and professional-looking necklace. This is a great project for a beginner.

SKILL Easy

MATERIALS
1 reel of 32 gauge silver jewelry wire
1 ounce (25g) of amethyst chip beads
1 tube of Gutermann Rocaille 9 seed beads, shade 1005
Barrel clasp

EQUIPMENT
Size C (2.75mm) crochet hook
Scissors

SIZE
One size

PREPARATION
First thread all the beads you will need onto the wire before you start to crochet. Thread one amethyst chip followed by two glass beads until you have a minimum of 54 amethyst chips and 108 seed beads. It doesn't matter whether a strand begins with an amethyst chip or a bead.

tip
You don't need wire cutters for this very fine wire; any ordinary pair of scissors will do.

It is worth threading more beads than you think you will need as you can always discard any you don't use and you will not be able to add more once you have started unless you cut the wire.

PATTERN
Make a slip knot.
This necklace is made very simply by crocheting a series of chains with a bead placed after every second chain.

After every second chain, slide a bead up the wire so that it is close to the last chain you made, then make another chain so that the bead is caught in the middle.

When the strand measures approximately 14in (35cm), cut the wire leaving a 4in (10cm) tail and with the hook, draw the end through the last chain.

Make four more strands like the first. Don't worry if the strands aren't exactly the same length. Slightly varying lengths will enhance the overall look.

FINISHING

Gather all five strands together, taking care not to twist them, and attach one half of the barrel clasp to each end by threading the strands through and winding them back on themselves, twisting several times. Cut the ends.

ring o' roses

A very pretty cuff bracelet using both wire and yarn techniques. Dainty yarn rosebuds are attached to a wire mesh bracelet for an arresting yet simple design. Alternatively, use the same rosebud to make a sweet hair slide.

SKILL Intermediate

MATERIALS
1 reel of 32 gauge silver jewelry wire
1 skein of DMC Mouliné 25, shade 321 (scarlet)
Silver popper

EQUIPMENT
Size A (2mm) hook
Size B (2.5mm) hook
Blunt-ended needle
Scissors

SIZES
Small – to fit wrists 6in (15cm)–6¾in (17cm)
Medium – to fit wrists 6¾in (17cm)–7½in (19cm)
Large – to fit wrists 7½ in (19cm)–8¼ in (21cm)

Instructions for the smallest size are given first, larger sizes are in brackets.

BRACELET

Using the size A (2mm) crochet hook and the jewelry wire, make a slip knot, leaving a 4in (10cm) tail. Make 6ch.
1st Row 1sc into 2nd ch from hook, 1sc into each ch to end, turn. (5 sts)
2nd Row 1ch, 1sc into each st to end, turn.
Repeat 2nd Row until bracelet fits your wrist with ⅝in (1.5cm) to spare. Fasten off, leaving a 4in (10cm) tail.

ROSEBUD

MAKE 5 (6, 6).
The petal effect of the rosebud is created by working outwards in a spiral and then working back into the center to give the flower texture.

Using the red yarn and the size B (2.25mm) crochet hook, make a slip knot.

Make 2ch.
1st Round work 6sc into 2nd ch from hook.
2nd Round 2sc into each sc to end. (12 sts)
3rd Round (1sc into each of next 3sc, 2sc into next sc) 3 times. (15 sts)
4th Round 1sc into each of next 6sc, 1sc around stem of next st, 1sc around stem of next st in row below, 1sc around stem of each of 6 sts in first row. Fasten off and pull tail through so it is now at the back of the bud.

FINISHING
At each end of the cuff, use the tail of the wire to attach the popper, making sure that you place each half of the popper on opposite sides of the cuff. Weave in the ends to secure.

Ensuring that the rosebuds are evenly spaced on the bracelet, secure each flower by pulling the tails through the mesh with a crochet hook and tying the ends in a knot. Sew the yarn back into the flower and fasten off.

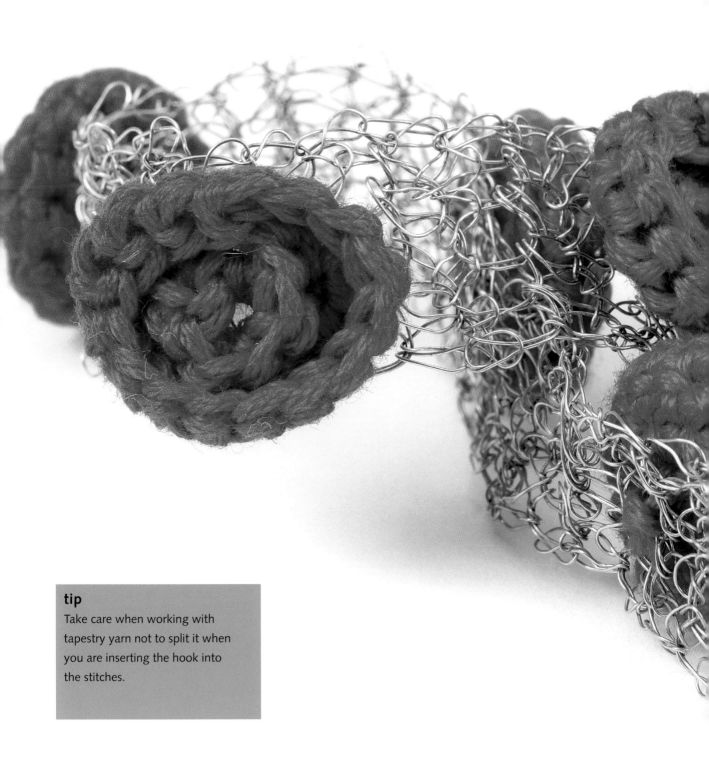

HAIR PIN

The tiny rosebuds are ideal for brightening a simple hair clip. Make a pair of leaves to complete the look.

MATERIALS

1 skein of DMC Mouliné 25, shade 992 (green)

1 skein of DMC Mouliné 25, shade 321 (scarlet)

EQUIPMENT

Size B (2.25mm) hook

Blunt-ended needle

Scissors

ROSEBUD

Make 1 rosebud in shade 321 as on p.38.

LEAVES

Using a size B (2.25mm) hook and shade 992, make a slip knot. Make 11ch.

1st Row sl st into 2nd ch from hook, 1hdc into next ch, 1dc into next ch, 1hdc into next ch, 1 sl st into each of next 2ch, 1hdc into next ch, 1 dc into next ch, 1 hdc into next ch, sl st into last chain. Fasten off.

FINISHING

Attach the flower to the leaves by drawing the tails
from the flower through the leaves and tying in a knot
to secure. To attach to a hair slide, simply slide the grip
through the center of the leaves as shown.

super hooper earrings

Create these fantastic dangly earrings in no time at all by crocheting wire and clusters of beads around two different size rings.

SKILL Easy

MATERIALS

2 x ¾in (19mm) brass rings (curtain accessories)

2 x 1in (25mm) brass rings

1 reel of 32 gauge silver jewelry wire

1 tube of Gutermann Rocaille 9 seed beads, shade 6510

1 pair of earrings hooks

EQUIPMENT

Size A (2mm) crochet hook

Flat-nosed pliers

Scissors

special terms

Scb This is one single crochet with a bead. To work a bead into the fabric, slide the required number of beads up the wire so they are close to the ring, insert the hook into the ring, yo, draw through a loop, yo, draw through two loops.

This pattern requires you to add 2, 3, 4, and 5 beads at a time. This will be described in the pattern as sc2b, sc3b, sc4b, and sc5b. These instructions are worked exactly the same as scb, but sliding more beads up the wire according to the instruction.

BEADING

Thread all the beads onto the wire first. For this project you will need approximately 14in (35cm) of beads for each earring. It is worth threading a few more beads than you think you will need as you will not be able to add more once you have started, unless you cut the wire.

PATTERN

Attach the earring hook to the smaller ring. You may need to use a pair of flat-nosed pliers to manipulate the earring hook.

Without making a slip knot and holding the smaller ring in front of the wire, between the thumb and middle finger of your left hand, insert the hook into the center of the ring, yo, draw the loop back through the ring, yo, draw through the loop on the hook.

Work alternately sc4b, sc2b around the ring, until you have worked 11 sts. This will take you halfway around the smaller ring.

Now you need to add the next ring, so, holding the larger ring between the thumb and middle finger of your left hand, insert the hook into the center of the ring, draw the loop back through the ring, yo, draw through both loops on the hook.

Work around this ring as with the smaller ring, working alternately sc5b, sc3b [see below], until you have worked 26 sts. This will take you all the way around the larger ring.

Rejoin to the smaller ring by working a sl st into the last st you made on the smaller ring (otherwise you will have a gap).

Continue to work around the smaller ring, working alternately sc4b, sc2b until you have worked a further 11 sts. Now join the ring by working a sl st into the first st. Cut the wire and weave in the ends.

Make another earring in exactly the same way.

finger crochet bracelets

Easy necklaces or bracelets with beads made using finger crochet.

SKILL Very easy

All you need is a little bit of yarn, some brightly colored beads and your fingers. It's that simple.

MATERIALS

2 x 47in (120cm) of dk or 4ply yarn or 47in (120cm) of ribbon for each bracelet

9 (10, 11) x ⅜in (1cm) diameter wooden beads in assorted colors

EQUIPMENT

Collapsible eye beading needle

Scissors

SIZES

Small – to fit wrists 6in (15cm)–6¾in (17cm)

Medium – to fit wrists 6¾in (17cm)–7½in (19cm)

Large – to fit wrists 7½in (19cm)–8¼in (21cm)

Instructions for the smallest size are given first, larger sizes are in brackets.

PATTERN

1 Take the ends of the yarn from both balls and, using a collapsible eye beading needle, thread 9 (10, 11) wooden beads. If you are working with lengths of yarn, you will need to secure the beads: holding both strands together, tie a knot at one end so the beads don't fall off, then thread the beads onto the yarn.

2 Wrap the yarn twice around your index finger as shown above.

3 Pull loop 1 (nearest your hand) over loop 2 (nearest your fingertip) and off your finger [see above]. You now have one loop remaining on your finger, which becomes loop 1.

4 Using the yarn from the ball, not the tail, wrap one more loop of yarn around your finger, creating a new loop 2.

5 Pull loop 1 over the new loop 2 and off your finger. Tighten the stitches as you go.

6 Slide a bead up close to the last stitch you made, wrap a loop around your finger, creating a new loop 2 [see left], and pull loop 1 over loop 2 and the bead [see lower left].

Repeat steps 4–6, adding a bead every other stitch until you have worked all the beads.

FINISHING

Cut the yarn, leaving a 6in (15cm) tail. Draw the end through the final loop and pull tight to secure. Tie the two ends together, ensuring that the bracelet is big enough to pass over your hand and fit around your wrist. Trim the excess yarn.

bead and wire amulet

A striking take on the traditional amulet, using bold metallic beads worked into a spiral plate and decorated with beaded fronds, the amulet is then suspended from a silver-plated chain.

SKILL Intermediate

MATERIALS

1 tube of Gutermann Rocaille 9 seed beads, shade 1005 (silver)

1 tube of Gutermann Rocaille 9 seed beads, shade 9625 (dark blue)

1 reel of 32 gauge silver jewelry wire

1 silver-plated chain necklace

1 silver jump ring

10 x 2in (5cm) head pins

EQUIPMENT

Size B (2.25mm) crochet hook

Scissors

Round-nosed pliers

SIZE

One size

special terms

Scb: This is one single crochet with a bead. To work a bead into the fabric, slide the bead up the wire so it is close to the fabric, insert the hook to the left of the bead into the next stitch, yo, draw through a loop, yo, draw through two loops. The bead will now be caught in the stitch.

tip

Double-check at each stage that you have got the correct amount of beads. If you have too many beads, you can always smash any you don't need with a pair of pliers, but if you have too few, you will need to start again.

PREPARATION

Threading the beads. The beads need to be threaded in the reverse order to the one in which they are used in the pattern. This pattern uses simple alternating rings of color; however, if you want to do a different color arrangement, chart your work first, and calculate the bead order in advance.

Thread in this order: 48 silver beads, 40 blue beads, 32 silver beads, 24 blue beads, 16 silver beads, 8 blue beads.

PATTERN

Make a slip knot.

Make 5ch, join in a ring with a sl st.

1st Round (right side) work 8scb into the center of the ring. (8 sts)

2nd Round 2scb into each scb of previous round. (16 sts)

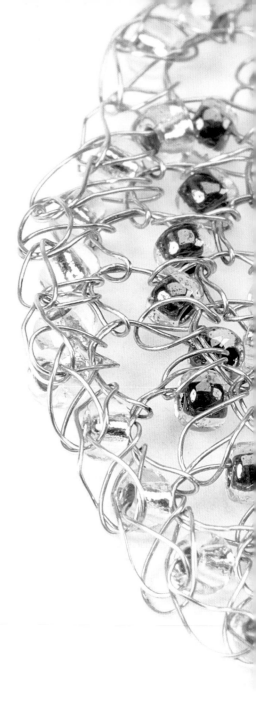

3rd Round *1scb into next st, 2scb into next st; rep from * to end. (24 sts)

4th Round *1scb into each of next 2 sts, 2scb into next st; rep from * to end. (32 sts)

5th Round *1scb into each of next 3 sts, 2scb into next st; rep from * to end. (40 sts)

6th Round *1scb into each of next 4 sts, 2scb into next st; rep from * to end, sl st into first st. (48 sts) Fasten off.

DANGLY FRONDS

Thread 25 silver beads onto a 2in (5cm) head pin that has a flattened end so that the beads won't slide off. With the right side of the amulet facing, pass the end of the pin through both loops of a selvedge stitch, opposite where you fastened off. Using a pair of round-nosed pliers, and starting at the tip of the pin, make a complete loop [see below].

Continue to add fronds into each stitch along the bottom until you have 10 fronds.

FINISHING

Attach a jump ring to the center point at the top of the amulet (the opposite side from the fronds). Pass the chain through it.

ribbon hair band

An elegant and sparkly hair band, dotted with beads and threaded through with a length of velvet ribbon. Perfect for sophisticated soirées!

SKILL Intermediate

MATERIALS

1 x 1 ounce (25g) ball of Anchor Arista, shade 340
1 yard (1m) of ⅝in (15mm) width black velvet ribbon
¼ ounce (10g) of ¼in (4mm) beads
Strong craft glue

EQUIPMENT

Size B (2.25mm) crochet hook
Collapsible eye beading needle
Scissors

SIZE

One size

PATTERN

Make a slip knot.
Make 138ch.

You are now creating the blocks that provide a frame into which you will weave the ribbon.
1st Row 1tr into 9th ch from hook, *2ch, skip 2ch, 1tr into next ch; rep from * to end, turn.

Decorative edging Simple shells worked round the outside give this band a pretty finish.
2nd Row 1ch, sl st into first tr, *4dc in 2ch sp, sl st with bead into next tr; rep from * to last block. Work 12dc into last block this will take you round to the other edge of the hair band. Now work 1sl st with a bead into base of first tr. Continue as before to work

special terms

Tr (triple crochet): Wrap the yarn around the hook twice, insert the hook into the work, yo, draw a loop through the work, yo, draw through the first two loops on the hook, yo, draw through the next two loops on the hook, yo, draw through the last two loops on the hook. You will be left with one loop on the hook.

Slip stitch with a bead: Slide the bead up the yarn so it is close to the fabric, insert the hook to the left of the bead and into the next stitch, yo, draw the hook through the fabric and the loop on the hook.

(4dc in 2ch sp, sl st with bead into base of next tr) until you reach the last block. Work 8dc into last block, finishing with a sl st into top of first tr. Fasten off.

FINISHING

Starting from the back, thread the velvet ribbon through the hair band. Finish the ribbon by folding the ends in half and making a cut as shown, open the ribbon up and seal the ends with glue or clear nail polish. Sew in all the ends.

foxy fire

Create this amazing-looking choker just by working silver wire in single crochet, incorporating hundreds of fiery beads of different shades. The choker is finished off with a hook and eye fastening.

SKILL Intermediate

MATERIALS

1 tube of Gutermann Rocaille 9 seed beads,
  shades 1850, 3565, 1245 and 4740
1 reel of 32 gauge silver jewelry wire
2 pairs of No.1 silver hooks and eyes

EQUIPMENT

Size B (2.25mm) crochet hook
Scissors

SIZE

This choker can be made to any size; measure against your neck as you go.

special terms

Scb This is one single crochet with a bead. To work a bead into the fabric: Slide the bead up the wire so it is close to the fabric, insert the hook to the left of the bead into next st, yo, draw through a loop, yo, draw through two loops. The bead will now be caught in the stitch.

Sc3b This is the same as scb, except you add three beads at a time.

Scb2tog A decrease of one stitch by working two stitches together, adding just one bead: Slide the bead up to the last st worked, insert the hook to the left of the bead and into the next st, yo, draw through a loop, insert the hook into next st, yo, draw through a loop, yo, draw through all three loops on the hook, leaving just one loop [see left].

In this pattern, as you are adding three beads to each stitch, the pattern instruction will read sc3b2tog, where only three beads are added across both stitches.

2sc3b An increase of one stitch by working 2sc into one stitch, adding three beads with each sc.

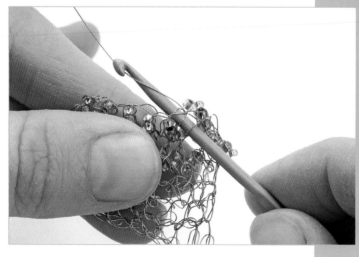

PREPARATION

Thread all the beads onto the wire first. To complete this project, you will need approximately 108in (275cm) of beads; this will be ample for any size.

PATTERN

Make a slip knot leaving an 8in (20cm) tail.
Make 11ch.
1st Row 1sc into 2nd ch from hook, 1sc into each ch to end, turn. (10 sts)
2nd Row 1ch, 1sc into each sc to end, turn. Rep 2nd row twice more.

This is just a guideline. This choker has a natural flowing look, so you can follow the pattern or go freestyle, alternately increasing and decreasing at the beginning and end of the row to create a wavy shape.

1st Row 1ch, sc3b2tog, 1sc3b into each of next 6 sts, sc3b2tog, turn. (8 sts)
2nd Row 1ch, sc3b2tog, 1sc3b into each of next 4 sts, sc3b2tog, turn. (6 sts)
3rd Row 1ch, 1sc3b into each st to end, turn.
4th Row 1ch, 2sc3b into first st, 1sc3b into each st to end, turn. (7 sts)
5th Row 1ch, 1sc3b into each st to last st, 2sc3b into last st, turn. (8 sts)
6th Row 1ch, 1sc3b into each st to last st, 2sc3b into last st, turn. (9 sts)

7th Row 1ch, 2sc3b into first st, 1sc3b into each st to end, turn. (10 sts)
8th Row 1ch, 2sc3b into first st, 1scb into each st to last st, 2sc3b into last st. (12 sts)
9th Row 1ch, 1sc3b into each st to end, turn.
10th Row 1ch, sc3b2tog, 1sc3b into each of next 8 sts, sc3b2tog, turn. (10 sts)

Repeat 1st–10th Rows of the pattern until the choker just fits around your neck. Now, without adding any beads, work 4 rows straight:
Next Row 1ch, 1sc into each scb to end, turn.
Next Row 1ch, 1sc into each sc to end, turn.
Repeat this row 2 more times. Fasten off leaving a long tail.

FINISHING

Using the long wire tails at each end, attach the hooks and eyes to correspond at each end of the choker. Weave in the ends.

> **tip**
> If you are not able to complete the pattern by the time the choker fits nearly around your neck, simply increase or decrease as appropriate until you have 10 sts across, then work four rows of sc so that both ends match.

gold cuff

This elegant cuff looks like a classic piece of jewelry, is easy to wear and very quick to make. The design is a simple shell pattern held in shape by wire, which is crocheted into the cuff in the last row.

SKILL Intermediate

MATERIALS

1 x 1 ounce (25g) ball of Twilleys Goldfingering in gold, shade 35

20in (50cm) of 20 gauge jewelry wire

1 gold bugle bead

Strong craft glue

EQUIPMENT

Size D (3.25mm) crochet hook

Blunt-ended needle

Scissors

Wire cutters

Pliers, any type

SIZE

This cuff can be made to any size. Measure against your wrist as you go.

PATTERN

Make a slip knot.

Make 11ch.

1st Row 1 shell into 8th ch from hook, skip 2ch, 1tr into last ch, turn.

2nd Row 5ch, skip 3 sts, 1 shell into next st, skip 2 sts, 1tr into 4th of 7ch at start of 1st Row, turn.

3rd Row 5ch, skip 3 sts, 1 shell into next st, skip 2 sts, 1tr into 4th of 5ch, turn.

Repeat 3rd Row until the cuff fits comfortably around your wrist with no overlap.

special terms

Shell The shell in this pattern is composed of five complete triple crochets worked into one stitch to create a shell or fan shape [see above].

Tr (triple crochet): Wrap the yarn around the hook twice, insert the hook into the work, yo, draw a loop through the work, yo, draw through first 2 loops on hook, yo, draw through the next 2 loops on the hook, yo, draw through the last 2 loops on the hook. You will be left with 1 loop on the hook.

1st Round 1ch, work 1 round of sc evenly around the edges of the cuff as follows: Work 4sc into first ch sp, *1 sc into next st, 2sc into next ch sp; rep from * to

tip

Before you start to work the wire into your bracelet, fold the ends of the wire over using a pair of pliers; this way the wire is less likely to be drawn into your work as you crochet around the cuff.

last ch sp on first side, 4sc into last ch sp, 3sc into base of shell, 4sc into next ch sp *1sc into next st, 2sc into next ch sp; rep from * until you reach the last ch sp, 4sc into last ch sp, 1sc into each of next 2 sts.

2nd Round Laying the wire alongside your work, 1sc around the wire into each sc to end.

FINISHING

Trim off any excess wire. Now put a dab of glue onto each end of the wire and insert into either side of a bead to secure. Sew in all the ends. You might need to shape the bangle so that it is symmetrical and fits nicely around your wrist.

hippy ring

A sweet flower-power ring made in contrasting sparkly shades. Worked in just two rounds, this is so quick even a beginner will be able to make this very simple ring.

SKILL Easy

MATERIALS

1 x 1 ounce (25g) ball of Twilleys Goldfingering, shade 60
1 x 1 ounce (25g) ball of Twilleys Goldfingering, shade 35
1 ring base
Strong craft glue

EQUIPMENT

Size A (2mm) crochet hook
Blunt-ended needle

SIZE

One size

PATTERN

Using shade 60, make a slip knot.
Make 4ch and join in a ring with a sl st.
1st Round 1ch, work 8sc into ring, join with a sl st into back loop of first sc.
2nd Round *3ch, 1 cluster, 3ch, sl st blo into same back loop, sl st blo into next st; rep from * to end, working last sl st into back of first sc from 1st Round. Fasten off.

Using shade 35, attach yarn to front loop of first sc in 1st Round. Work 1sc flo into each st in 1st Round. Sl st flo into first sc. Fasten off.

special terms

flo (front loop only): Work the stitch in the normal way, but inserting the hook under the front loop only of each stitch.
blo (back loop only): Work the stitch in the normal way, but inserting the hook under the back loop only of each stitch.

Cluster: This cluster is composed of three double crochets worked into the same stitch, leaving the last loop of each stitch on the hook; when all three double crochets have been worked, yo, and draw through all four loops on the hook.

FINISHING

Sew in all the ends.
Place a dab of glue on the ring base and press the flower firmly into place.

diamond life earrings

Elegant wire mesh earrings worked into a diamond shape glittered with silvery beads.

SKILL Intermediate

MATERIALS

1 tube of Gutermann Rocaille 9 seed beads, shade 1005

1 reel of 32 gauge silver jewelry wire

1 pair of earring hooks

EQUIPMENT

Size A (2mm) crochet hook

Flat-nosed pliers

Scissors

PREPARATION

First, thread on all of the beads you will need for each earring; if you run out of beads you will need to cut the wire and add some more, so it is always worth adding more than you think you will need. You will need to thread on approximately 5in (13cm) of beads (or 75 beads) for each earring.

special terms

Scb: This is one single crochet with a bead. To work a bead into the fabric, slide the bead up the wire so it is close to the fabric, insert hook to the left of the bead and into next stitch, yo, draw through a loop, yo, draw through 2 loops. The bead will now be caught in the stitch.

Scb2tog A decrease of 1 st by working 2 sts together, adding just 1 bead. Slide the bead up to the last st worked, insert the hook into the next st, yo, draw through a loop, insert the hook into the next st, yo, draw through a loop, yo, draw through all 3 loops on hook, leaving just 1 loop.

Scb3tog A decrease of 2 sts by working 3 sts together, adding just 1 bead. Slide the bead up to the last st worked, insert the hook into the next st, yo, draw through a loop, insert the hook into the next st, yo, draw through a loop, yo, insert the hook into the next st, yo, draw through a loop, yo, draw through all 4 loops on hook, leaving just 1 loop [see left].

Note on increasing (working 2 or more stitches in the same place): Add a bead for each stitch you work, so an increase of 1 stitch will have 2 beads.

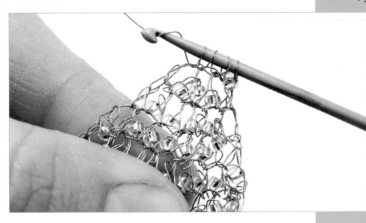

There is no right or wrong side. The beads are added to every row and can be seen equally from both sides.

PATTERN

Starting at the top of the earring, make a slip knot. Make 2ch.

1st Row 1scb in 2nd ch from hook, turn.

2nd Row 1ch, 3scb into the st, turn.

3rd Row 1ch, 2scb into first st, 1scb into next st, 2scb into final st, turn. (5 sts)

Cont to work in single crochet adding a bead in each st and increasing by 1 st at each end of every row until there are 11 sts.

Next Row 1ch, 1scb into each st to end, turn.

Next Row 1ch, scb2tog, 1scb into each of next 7 sts, scb2tog, turn. (9 sts)

Continue to work in single crochet, adding a bead in each st and decreasing by 1 st at each end of every row until 3 sts remain.

Next Row 1ch, scb3tog, turn.

Next Row 1ch, 1scb into final st. Fasten off.

FINISHING

Weave the wire ends into the mesh and cut. Add an earring hook to the top of earring. You may need to use the pliers to open and close the wire loop that attaches to the diamond.

tip

Working with wire can be difficult, and the wire may not behave in the way that yarn does. You should be familiar with the appearance of crocheted fabric so that you can find the stitches more easily.

Always work under a bright light; it can be hard to see what you are doing with wire.

bang bangles

Create cool and unusual bangles in record time. Using any yarn you like –
chunky, fine, sparkly, or fluffy – simply crochet around a plain metal bangle. You
can make your bangles all the same color or mix and match with a variety. Each
bangle uses only a small amount of yarn, so one ball of yarn will make dozens of
bangles; alternatively, it is a great way of using up odds and ends.

SKILL Easy

MATERIALS
1 x 2 ounce (50g) ball of yarn – **Twilleys Goldfingering**
   yarns or other Lurex-type metallic yarns: sea green
   (shade 66), non-metallic silver (57),
   sparkly pink (62), sparkly black (31), sparkly purple (60),
   sparkly light blue (53); **Pink fluffy:** Wendy Jazz
   in Memphis; **Black:** RYC Cashsoft dk in Black;
   Blue wool: Colinette point 5 in Neptune
¼in (4mm) silver beads
Plain metal bangles

EQUIPMENT
Blunt-ended needle
Size D (3.25mm) crochet hook
Scissors

SIZE
One size

This is a very simple project – just one round of single
crochet worked tightly all around the bangle.

PATTERN
Make a slip knot.
Hold the bangle in front of the yarn, between the
thumb and middle finger of your left hand. Insert the
hook into the ring, wrap the yarn around the hook,
draw the loop through the ring, yo, draw through the
loop on the hook [see below].

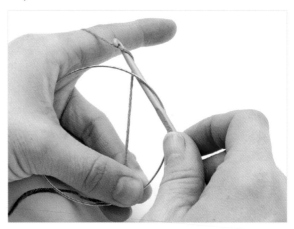

Insert the hook into the ring again, yo, draw the
loop through the ring, yo, draw the hook through
both loops on the hook—this will leave one loop. This
makes one single crochet.

Continue to work around the bangle in single
crochet until you have worked as many stitches as you
can fit; this will make the yarn twist and buckle to give
it a wavy look. You may need to push up the stitches
you have made to allow you more room.

Beaded bangles

For an original twist why not add beads to your bangle? Thread all the beads for the project in advance and add one bead after every few stitches. In the bangle shown below right, a bead was added to every fourth stitch with the scb technique (see p.56), using a total of 30 beads.

FINISHING

Fasten off by cutting the yarn, making 1 chain, then drawing the tail through the chain. Now pull tight. Sew in the ends. Arrange the yarn so that it is twisted evenly around the bangle.

simple bead necklaces

These sweet necklaces couldn't be simpler to make and are an ideal project for a complete beginner. Just by following a few simple steps you can create beautiful jewelry in literally minutes!

SKILL Very easy

MATERIALS

1 tube of Gutermann Rocaille 9 seed beads, shades 7300, 7230, and 1005

1 x 2 ounces (50g) ball of DMC Babylo 10 (8 crochet yarn, shade 482

2 crimps per necklace

1 barrel clasp per necklace

EQUIPMENT

Size B (2.25mm) crochet hook

Flat-nosed pliers

Collapsible eye beading needle

Scissors

SIZE

These can be made to any size; measure against your neck as you go.

BEAD CHAIN

This is the most straightforward bead necklace; it is simply a chain of crochet, with a bead after each stitch. Make even stitches to keep your work tight.

Using bead shade 7300, thread approximately 150 beads onto the yarn (this is about 10in/25cm of beads) using the beading needle; this will be ample for any size. It is important you thread all the beads you will need (and a few more just in case) before you

start making your necklace. To add more, you would need to cut the yarn, which would spoil the look of this simple chain.

MAKE A SLIP KNOT

Make a loop near the end of the yarn, leaving a 4in (10cm) tail. Now insert the hook into the loop from front to back and draw another loop through it. Pull the knot close to the hook, but not too tight.

MAKING CHAINS

This necklace is made very simply by a series of chains with a bead added after every chain. To make a chain (ch), wrap the yarn around the hook from back to front and draw it through the loop on the hook. This makes one chain stitch.

You might want to practice making a few chains until you have a nice, smooth action.

ADDING BEADS

Once you have mastered the chain stitch, you are ready to make your necklace. Slide a bead up the yarn, close to the slip knot, wrap the yarn around the hook, and draw it through the loop on the hook, making a chain stitch. Continue in this way, bringing a bead up the yarn, then working a chain stitch until the necklace is long enough to fit comfortably around your neck.

FINISHING

Cut the yarn, leaving a 4in (10cm) tail and draw the end through the last chain.

At each end, using the beading needle, thread on the crimp, then the barrel clasp, now pass the needle back through the crimp. Crush the crimp with the pliers to secure the yarn and cut the yarn off close to the crimp.

PETAL CHAIN

This is a variation on the bead chain. Again, the necklace is worked as just one chain, but instead of inserting a bead into each stitch, you will be making a series of small loops with beads.

Using bead shade 7230, thread on approximately 150 beads – this will be about 10in (25cm) of beads.

Make a slip knot.
Make 6ch.
Now slide 4 beads up the yarn, close to the last st you made, insert the hook into the 3rd ch from the hook (not counting the ch on the hook), wrap the yarn around the hook, draw through a loop, wrap the yarn around the hook, draw through 2 loops. This is 1 single crochet.

Continue in this way, working *6ch, adding 4 beads, then working 1sc into the 3rd ch from the hook; rep from * until the necklace is long enough to fit comfortably around your neck, ending with 6ch. Finish off as for the bead chain.

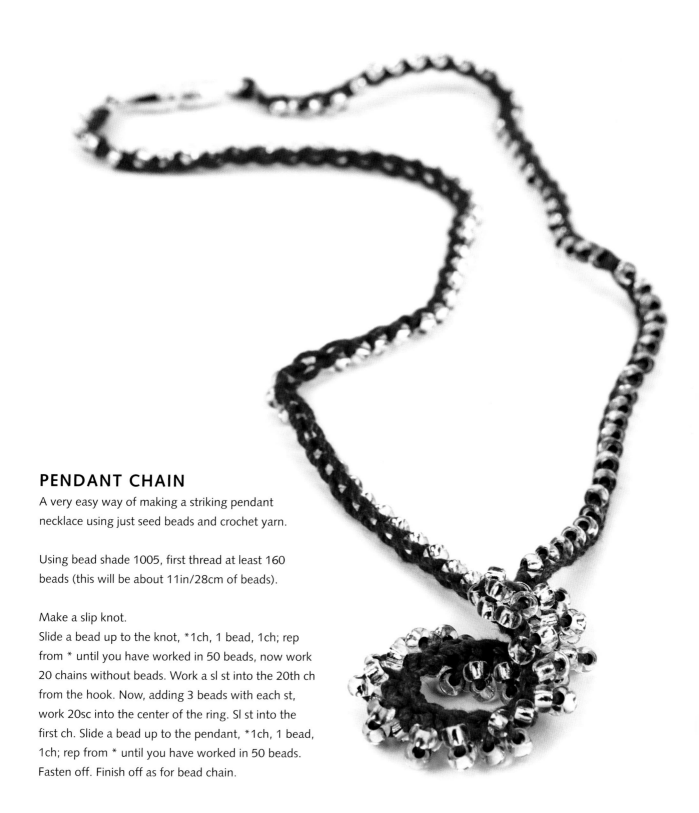

PENDANT CHAIN

A very easy way of making a striking pendant necklace using just seed beads and crochet yarn.

Using bead shade 1005, first thread at least 160 beads (this will be about 11in/28cm of beads).

Make a slip knot.
Slide a bead up to the knot, *1ch, 1 bead, 1ch; rep from * until you have worked in 50 beads, now work 20 chains without beads. Work a sl st into the 20th ch from the hook. Now, adding 3 beads with each st, work 20sc into the center of the ring. Sl st into the first ch. Slide a bead up to the pendant, *1ch, 1 bead, 1ch; rep from * until you have worked in 50 beads. Fasten off. Finish off as for bead chain.

striped bead earrings

Make cool, dangly earrings with crocheted balls mixed with beads. You can add as many as you like and mix with any beads you like – just make sure not to make them too heavy!

SKILL Easy

MATERIALS

DMC Mouliné 25 yarn, shade 125

Small bag of polyester filling or cotton wool

6 x Gutermann ⅓in (8mm) glass beads in black, shade 1000

4 x Gutermann Rocaille 9 seed beads, shade 7300

1 pair of earring hooks

2 jump rings

EQUIPMENT

Size B (2.25mm) hook

Collapsible eye beading needle

Blunt-ended needle

Sharp needle

Scissors

GAUGE

Small balls should measure about ¾in (2cm) in diameter.
Large balls should measure about 1in (2.5cm) in diameter.

It doesn't matter if you don't stick exactly to these measurements, but you want to ensure that you work to the same gauge for both earrings otherwise they will look uneven.

tip
Mark the beginning of each round with a piece of colored thread to avoid losing your place.

SMALL BALL – MAKE 2

Make a slip knot.

Make 2ch.

1st Round work 8sc into 2nd ch from hook.

2nd Round 2sc into each sc to end. (16 sts)

3rd and 4th Rounds 1sc into each sc to end.

Place filling into the ball.

5th Round (sc2tog) 8 times. (8 sts)

6th Round 1sc into each sc to end.

Fasten off. Sew in the ends.

LARGE BALL – MAKE 2

Make a slip knot.

Make 2ch.

1st Round work 8sc into 2nd ch from hook.

2nd Round 2sc into each sc to end. (16 sts)

3rd Round *1sc into each of the next 3sc, 2sc into next sc; rep from * to end. (20 sts)

4th Round 1sc into each sc to end.

5th Round as 4th round.

6th Round *1sc into each of next 3sc, sc2tog into next sc; rep from * to end. (16 sts)

7th Round (sc2tog) 8 times. (8 sts)

8th Round 1sc into each sc to end.

Fasten off. Sew in the ends.

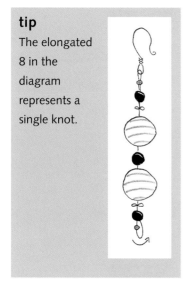

tip
The elongated
8 in the
diagram
represents a
single knot.

FINISHING

Cut an 8in (20cm) piece of the yarn and thread it onto a sharp needle (a sharp needle will pass through the stuffing more easily), pass it through the smaller of the two beads; now, using the beading needle (assuming the bead won't pass over the regular needle), thread one ⅓in (8mm) bead, again using the sharp needle, thread the second crochet ball. Now, using the big eye needle, thread one more ⅓in (8mm) bead followed by one seed bead. Pass the yarn back through the ⅓in

8mm bead and tie a knot between the larger crochet ball and the ⅓in (8mm) bead.

Pull the other end of the yarn firmly so that the balls and the beads are now snug. Thread one ⅓in (8mm) bead and one seed bead and the earring hook, pull the yarn firmly so the beads are snug with no gaps between them, now pass the yarn back through the seed bead and ⅓in (8mm) bead and secure with a knot between the smaller crochet ball and the ⅓in (8mm) bead. Sew in all the ends.

bead and mesh cuff bracelets

These pretty cuff bracelets are created using wire worked into a mesh with beads added for decoration. You can add the beads in any design you like by following a simple chart like the one given here, or make up your own.

SKILL Easy

The technique used here is simply double crochet fabric; however, you should be familiar with the appearance of regular yarn fabric before attempting this project as the stitches can be a little hard to identify at first.

MATERIALS

1 reel of 32 gauge silver jewelry wire

1 tube of Gutermann Rocaille 9 seed beads, shade 7300

1 tube of Gutermann Rocaille 9 seed beads, shade 4740

1 tube of Gutermann Facon star sequins shade, 9912

1 silver popper for each cuff (except sequin cuff)

EQUIPMENT

Size B (2.25mm) crochet hook (bead cuffs)

Size K (6.5mm) crochet hook (sequin cuff)

Scissors

SIZES

Small – to fit wrists 6in (15cm)–6¾in (17cm)

Medium – to fit wrists 6¾in (17cm)–7½in (19cm)

Large – to fit wrists 7½in (19cm)–8¼in (21cm)

Instructions for the smallest size are given first, larger sizes are in brackets.

BEAD STRIPE BRACELET

Create a striped pattern by working a row of beads (shade 4740) on every right side row.

You will need approximately 80 (90, 100) beads. Thread these directly onto the wire before you start to crochet.

PATTERN

Using a size B (2.25mm) hook, make a slip knot, leaving a 4in (10cm) tail.

Make 6ch.

1st Row (right side) 1sc into 2nd ch from hook, 1sc into each ch to end, turn. (5 sts)

tip

You may want to add a few more beads in case you have miscounted. Any beads you don't use can be discarded at the end.

2nd Row 1ch, 1sc into each st to end, turn.
3rd and 4th Rows as 2nd row.
Next Row 1ch, 1scb into each sc to end, turn.
Next Row 1ch, 1sc into each scb to end, turn.

Repeat last 2 rows until bracelet just fits around your wrist, then repeat 2nd Row 4 times. Fasten off leaving a 4in (10cm) tail.

FINISHING

At each end, use the tail to attach the popper, making sure that you place the each half of the popper on opposite sides of the cuff. Weave in the ends to secure.

BEAD CLUSTER BRACELET

Similar to the striped design, this time arranging the beads (shade 7300) in clusters of four. A single crochet with four beads worked into it will be described as sc4b.

You will need approximately 112 (124, 136) beads. Thread these onto the wire.

PATTERN

Using a size B (2.25mm) hook, make a slip knot, leaving a 4in (10cm) tail.

Make 6ch.

1st Row 1sc into 2nd ch from hook, 1sc into each ch to end, turn. (5 sts)

2nd Row 1ch, 1sc into each st to end, turn.

3rd and 4th Rows as 2nd Row.

Next Row 1ch, 1sc into each of next 2sc, 1sc4b into next sc, 1sc into last 2sc, turn.

Next Row 1ch, 1sc into each st to end, turn.

Next Row 1ch, 1sc4b into first sc, 1sc into each of next 3sc, 1sc4b into last sc, turn.

Next Row 1ch, 1sc into each st to end, turn.

Repeat the last 4 rows until bracelet just fits around your wrist, then repeat 2nd Row 4 times. Fasten off, leaving a 4in (10cm) tail.

See bead stripe bracelet for notes on finishing.

CHARTS

You can create a bead chart like the one below. You might find this easier to follow than a pattern. This is the chart for the bead cluster bracelet.

It is important to note that the beads will be on whichever side you are working, so you might want to add beads only onto the right side of the mesh.

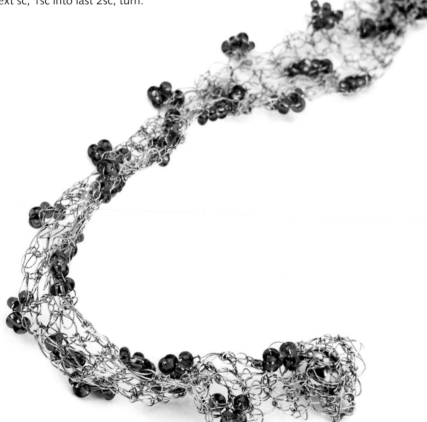

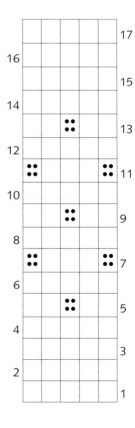

GIANT MESH SEQUIN BRACELET

A larger hook creates a lovely open, lacy mesh. Add giant multicolored star sequins for a really pretty and unusual bracelet. The fabric is too loose for a popper; instead, join the ends to make a complete ring. This open mesh has lots of stretch so it will easily fit over a hand.

Thread 14 sequins onto the wire (you may not need all of these). Add 1 randomly placed sequin to every right side row.

PATTERN

Using a size K (6.5mm) hook, make a slip knot, leaving a 4in (10cm) tail.

Make 5ch.

1st Row (wrong side): 1sc into 2nd ch from hook, 1sc into each ch to end, turn. (4 sts)

2nd Row (right side): Add 1 sequin placed randomly to this row. 1ch, 1sc into each st to end, turn.

3rd Row No sequin this row. 1ch, 1sc into each sc to end, turn.

Repeat 2nd and 3rd Rows until bracelet fits comfortably around your wrist, ending with a right side row.

FINISHING

Fold bracelet gently in half (without crushing) with right sides facing inwards. Join the two ends by working 1 row of sl st across each st. Fasten off, weave in the ends.

tubular necklace and bracelet

Dress to excess and relive the big-shouldered power-dressing chic of the Eighties with this tubular jewelry in sparkly yarn! This necklace, tipped with beads, looks great snaked around the neck. It's very simple to make, worked in a spiral without increases or decreases.

SKILL Easy

TUBE NECKLACE

MATERIALS
1 x 1 ounce (25g) ball of Anchor Arista shade 328
24in (60cm) of 18 gauge jewelry wire
Nylon thread
1 tube of Gutermann Rocaille 9 seed beads, shade 4740

EQUIPMENT
Size D (3.25mm) crochet hook
Blunt-ended needle
Round-nosed pliers
Scissors

SIZE
This can be made to any size, measure against your neck as you go.

PATTERN
Leaving an 8in (20cm) tail, make a slip knot.
Make 6ch, join in a ring with a sl st.
1st Round work 10sc into center of ring.
2nd Round 1sc into each sc to end.
Repeat 2nd Round until necklace fits comfortably around your neck and overlaps by at least 4in (10cm). It doesn't matter if you have not reached the end of the round. After the first couple of rounds, you won't

be able to keep track of where the round begins and ends, and in any case, it won't show [see above]. Fasten off, leaving an 8in (20cm) tail.

FINISHING
Using the tail, sew up one of the ends firmly so that the wire will not be able to poke through. Using the pliers, fold over the ends of the wire to create a rounded end and feed it into the necklace. Now sew up the other end.

Using nylon thread, as it is all but invisible, sew the beads onto each end of the necklace in an irregular pattern, applying two at a time. Sew in all the ends.

Gently manipulate the wired tube to fit around your neck.

TUBE BRACELET

MATERIALS
1 x 1 ounce (25g) ball of Anchor Arista, shade 332
6in (15cm) of ⅕in (1mm) jewelry wire

EQUIPMENT
As for tube necklace

SIZE
This can be made to any size, measure against your wrist
as you go.

PATTERN
Leaving an 8in (20cm) tail, make a slip knot.
Make 5ch, join in a ring with a sl st.
1st Round work 8sc into center of ring.

2nd Round 1sc into each sc to end.
Repeat 2nd Round until bracelet just fits around your
wrist. Fasten off leaving an 8in (20cm) tail.

FINISHING
Using the tail, sew up one of the ends firmly so that
the wire will not be able to poke through. Using the
pliers, fold over the ends of the wire to create a
rounded end and feed it into the bracelet. Now sew
up the other end. Sew in all the ends.

tip
It is quite easy to skip or add a stitch. So make sure
you count your stitches regularly to save having to
undo your work.

multicolored bead ring

A cool bead band ring in multicolored hues with beads worked into both sides of the fabric. So easy, it takes only minutes to make.

SKILL Easy

MATERIALS
1 tube of multicolored ¼in (5mm) glass beads
1 reel of 32 gauge silver jewelry wire

EQUIPMENT
Size C (2.75mm) crochet hook
Scissors

SIZES – SMALL, MEDIUM, LARGE
Instructions for the smaller size are given first, larger sizes are in brackets. *See p. 76.*

special terms
Scb This is one single crochet with a bead. To work a bead into the fabric, slide the bead up the wire so it is close to the fabric, insert hook to the left of the bead and into next stitch, yo, draw through a loop, yo, draw through 2 loops. The bead will now be caught in the stitch.

PREPARATION
Thread on 36 (39, 42) multicolored beads in any order.

PATTERN
Make a slip knot.
Make 4ch.
1st Row 1scb into 2nd ch from hook, 1scb into each of next 2ch, turn. (3 sts)
2nd Row 1ch, 1scb into each st to end, turn.
Repeat 2nd Row until the band just fits around your finger. Do not fasten off.

FINISHING
As the beads are on both sides of the mesh, there is no right or wrong side. Carefully fold the band in half so that the two ends are aligned. Work 1 row of sl st across the ends. Fasten off. Weave in all ends.

gold chain belt

This stunning gold chain belt uses a very simple technique called double chain, with pendant beads worked in. Finished with a hook, it can be worn as tight or loose as you like.

MATERIALS
1 x 1 ounce (25g) ball of Twilleys Goldfingering – gold, shade 4
1 ounce (25g) of large mixed glass beads, red
Small hook (of hook and eye set)

EQUIPMENT
Size B (2.25mm) crochet hook
Round-nosed pliers

SIZES
Small – 38in (96cm) – actual length of belt
Medium/large – 45in (115cm)

special terms
Dch (double chain): Make a single crochet, *insert hook under left loop of the stitch you have just made, yo and draw through a loop, yo, draw through 2 loops; this is one dch. Repeat from * until chain is required length.

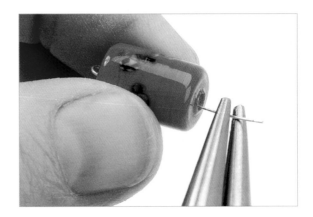

PREPARATION – MAKING PENDANT BEADS
So that the beads hang nicely from the chain, instead of threading them directly onto the yarn, they will be suspended on a short length of wire.

For each bead, cut a piece of wire approximately 1¾ in (3cm) length (you may need to use a shorter or longer piece of wire depending on the size of your bead). Using a pair of round-nosed pliers, make a small loop at one end; this is to ensure the bead doesn't slip off. Slip the bead onto the wire and at the other end, make a slightly larger loop for the yarn to pass through and poke the end of the wire back through the bead.

Thread on 25 (30) beads.

PATTERN
Make a slip knot, incorporating the first bead. Make 2ch.

1sc into 2nd ch from hook. Work 10dch, slide a bead up the yarn so it is close to your work. You might find it helpful to tuck it behind the work so that it doesn't

get in the way. Continue to work 10dch, 1 bead, until you have reached the last bead. Work 10 more dch, fasten off.

FINISHING

To complete the belt, simply sew a hook (from a hook and eye set) to the end of the belt. This can then be hooked anywhere along the length of the belt for a tight or relaxed look. Sew in any remaining ends.

tip
If you prefer, you can buy beads that already come in a wire cage with a loop for threading.

tumbling tendrils earrings

Striking and elegant earrings made from tumbling tendrils of sparkly bronze yarn crocheted in differing length spirals. The swirl effect is created by increasing by the same amount into each stitch forcing the fabric to create this fabulous twisted effect.

SKILL Easy

MATERIALS
1 x 1 ounce (25g) ball of Arista Anchor, shade 314, or
  other Lurex-type metallic yarn
1 pair of earring hooks

EQUIPMENT
Size B (2.25mm) crochet hook
Flat-nosed pliers
Blunt-ended needle
Scissors

PATTERN

FIRST TENDRIL
Make a slip knot.
Make 25ch.
Inserting hook into 4th ch from hook, work 3 dc.
Work 4dc into each ch to last ch but one.

SECOND TENDRIL
Without fastening off, make 30ch.
Inserting hook into 4th ch from hook, work 3 dc.
Work 4dc into each ch to 2nd ch from end, work 1dc, 1hdc, 1sc, 1sl st into next ch, leaving last ch unworked.

FINISHING
Fasten off and sew in the ends. Attach an earring hook to the center of the two tendrils. You may need to use a pair of pliers to open and firmly close the connecting ring on the earring hook.

tip
Always insert the hook under 2 strands of the base chain and make sure the base chain doesn't get twisted as this will create a slightly uneven look.

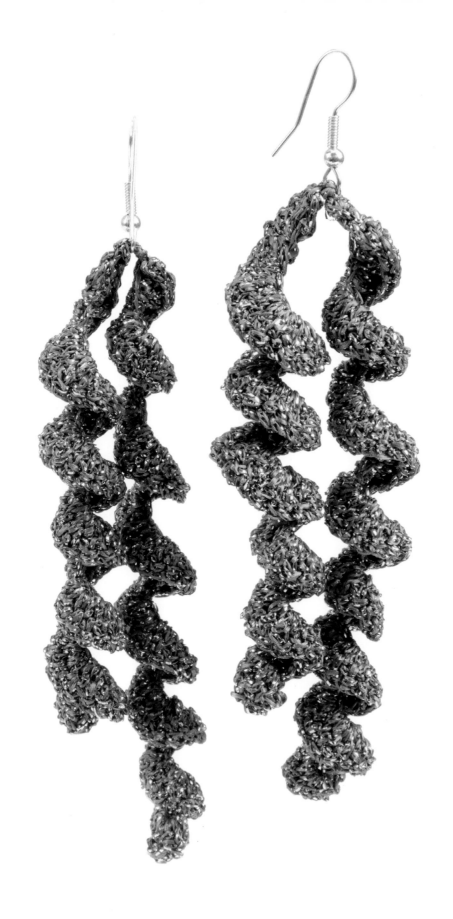

swirl brooch with pompoms

This cute brooch would look great worn on a coat or jacket for a new take on the wintry pompom. The swirl brooch is made by working lots of increases which create this amazing texture.

SKILL Easy

MATERIALS

1 x 2 ounce (50g) ball of Rowan RYC Cashsoft DK in lime

A piece of cardboard 4in (10cm) x 2in (5cm) for the pompoms

Silver pin back

Strong craft glue

EQUIPMENT

Size F (3.75mm) crochet hook

Blunt-ended needle

Scissors

BROOCH

Make a slip knot.

Make 6ch, join in a ring with a sl st.

1st Round work 15sc into ring.

2nd Round 3ch (count as 1dc), 2dc into base of 3ch, 3dc into each sc, ending with a sl st into top of 3ch. (45 sts)

3rd Round 3ch (count as 1dc), 2dc into base of 3ch, 3dc into each dc, ending with a sl st into top of 3ch. (135 sts)

4th Round As 3rd Round. (405 sts) Fasten off.

POMPOMS – MAKE 2

Cut two identical discs of cardboard measuring 2in (5cm) in diameter. Cut a ¾in (2cm) diameter hole in the center of both discs.

Place the discs together and, passing the yarn through the center of the hole, wrap the yarn around the outside of the discs. You will not be able to get the whole ball through the center of the disc, so cut off a length of yarn, wind this into a small ball and work with that. You can always add more yarn if you need it. When the cardboard is generously covered (so that it has a padded look), cut the yarn at the edge of the discs. Take a piece of yarn 20in (50cm) long and, leaving one short tail and one long, wrap it very tightly around the cut pieces in between the two discs and tie a knot. Remove the cardboard discs and fluff out your pompom.

Make a slip knot as close as you can to the pompom. Make 15ch. Fasten off.

FINISHING

Attach both pompoms to the swirl brooch. Sew in all the ends. Using strong craft glue, fix the pin back to the back of the swirl.

sparkly flower corsage

A fabulous flower corsage in contrasting sparkly yarns, worked with two sets of petals for an amazing three-dimensional look.

SKILL Intermediate

MATERIALS
1 x 1 ounce (25g) ball Twilleys Goldfingering – pink, shade 59

1 x 1 ounce (25g) ball Twilleys Goldfingering – black, shade 31

¾in (10mm) pin back

EQUIPMENT
Size B (2.25mm) crochet hook

Blunt-ended needle

Strong craft glue

Scissors

special terms
flo (front loop only): Work the stitch in the normal way, but inserting the hook under the front loop only of each st.

blo (back loop only): Work the stitch in the normal way, but inserting the hook under the back loop only of each st.

PATTERN
Work the central part of the flower in a spiral – this is a quicker way of working, but you will need to count your stitches as you go, or place a piece of yarn to mark the beginning of the row.

Using the black yarn, make a slip knot.
Make 2ch.

1st Round (right side) work 8sc in 2nd ch from hook.

2nd Round 2sc into each sc to end. (16 sts)

3rd Round *1sc into next sc, 2sc into next sc; rep from * to end of round. (24 sts)

4th Round *1sc into each of next 2sc, 2sc into next sc; rep from * to end of round. (32 sts)

5th Round *1sc into each of next 3sc, 2sc into next sc; rep from * to end of round (40 sts). Do not fasten off.

With RS facing, attach the pink yarn into the front loop of the next st.

FRONT PETAL
To make the front set of petals, work into the front loop only of each st.

1st Row 1sc flo into each of the next 7 sts, turn.

2nd Row 1ch, 1sc into each sc to end, turn.

3rd Row 1ch, 2sctog, 1sc into each sc to end, turn. Repeat 3rd Row until 1 st remains, turn.

Next Row 1ch, 1sc into remaining sc.

Working down the left side of the petal (RS facing), 1sc into each row end (8 sts), sl st flo into next st. Make 4 more petals as the first.

BACK PETALS
Using the pink yarn, sl st across the back of the next 4 sts.

1st Row 1sc into the back loop only of each of the next 7 sts, turn.

2nd–3rd Rows 1ch, 1sc into each sc to end, turn.

4th Row 1ch, 2sctog, 1sc into each sc to end, turn. Repeat 4th Row until 2 sts remain, turn.

Next Row 1ch, 1sc into each sc to end, turn.

Next Row 1ch, 2sctog, turn.

Next Row 1ch, 1sc into remaining sc.

Working down the left side of each petal, 1sc into each row end (10 sts), sl st blo into next st.

Make 4 more petals as the first.

BLACK BORDER FOR FRONT PETALS

Attach the black yarn to the sl st in between 2 front petals.

Working up the right side of the first petal, work into the row ends as follows: 1sc into end of 1st Row, 2sc into end of next row, 2hdc into end of next row, 2dc into end of next row, 2dc into end of next row, 2hdc into end of next row, 2sc into end of next row, 2sc into end of next row. Now work into sts down other side of petal as follows: 1ch, 2sc into next st, 2sc into next st, 2hdc into next st, 2dc into next st, 2dc into next st, 2hdc into next st, 2sc into next st, 1sc into next st.

Repeat for each petal. Fasten off.

BLACK BORDER FOR BACK PETALS

Attach the black yarn to the 2nd sl st in between 2 back petals.

Working up the right side of the first petal, work into each row end as follows: 1sc into end of 1st Row, 2sc into end of next row, 2hdc into end of next row, 2dc into end of next row, 2dc into end of next row, 2dc into end of next row, 2hdc into end of next row, 2sc into end of next row, 2sc into end of next row, 1sc into end of next row. Now work into sts down other side of petal as follows: 1ch, 2sc into next st, 2sc into next st, 2hdc into next st, 2dc into next st, 2dc into next st, 2dc into next st, 2hdc into next st, 2sc into next st, 2sc into next st, 1sc into next st.

Repeat for each petal. Sl st into next st. Fasten off.

FINISHING

Attach the pin back with a dab of glue or secure with the ends. Sew in all the ends.

love heart earrings

These funky heart-shaped earrings are very simple to make, using only very small quantities of yarn and finished with a round of sparkling beads. So quick and simple you'll be able to whip them up in no time at all for a night out.

SKILL Easy

MATERIALS
1 pair of earring hooks

1 x 1 ounce (25g) ball of Twilleys Goldfingering, shade 59

1 tube of Gutermann Rocaille 9 seed beads, shade 4965

1 reel of 32 gauge silver jewelry wire

EQUIPMENT
Size B (2.25mm) crochet hook

Blunt-ended needle

Scissors

special terms
scb: This is one single crochet with a bead. To work a bead into the fabric, slide the bead up the yarn so it is close to the fabric, insert hook to the left of the bead and into next stitch, yo, draw through a loop, yo, draw through 2 loops. The bead will now be caught in the stitch.

PATTERN
Using the Goldfingering and size B (2.25mm) crochet hook, make a slip knot.

Make 17ch.

1st Row 1sc in 2nd ch from hook and in each of next 6ch, skip 2ch, 1sc into each of next 7ch, turn. (14 sts)

2nd Row 1ch, 2sc in first sc, 1sc in each of next 5sc, skip 2ch, 1sc in each of next 5sc, 2sc in last sc, turn.

3rd and 4th Rows as 2nd row.

5th Row 1sc in each of next 6sc, skip 2sc, 1sc in each of next 6sc, turn. (12 sts)

6th Row 1ch, sc2tog, 1sc in each of next 3sc, skip 2ch, 1sc in each of next 3sc, sc2tog.

Thread the beads onto the wire before crocheting. You will need approximately 38 beads for each earring.

Bead Edging: Without turning, attach the wire into the next st, and work 1 round of sc around the heart as follows: 1scb into each row end, 1scb into the back of each ch, 3scb into 2ch space at the bottom center, 1scb into the back of each ch, 1scb into each row end, 1scb into each of next 4sc, skip 2sc, 1scb into each of next 4scb, sl st into first scb. Fasten off.

FINISHING
Sew in the ends and attach an earring hook to the center of each heart.

striped cuffs

Simple yet striking cuffs in two striped variations. These are really simple to crochet and can be made to fit any wrist size. As one ball of each color will make lots of cuffs, why not make a cuff for a friend?

SKILL Intermediate (for both styles)

WAVE CUFF

MATERIALS:

1 x 1 ounce (25g) ball of Twilleys Goldfingering in turquoise, shade 53

1 x 1 ounce (25g) ball of Twilleys Goldfingering in dark blue, shade 55

EQUIPMENT

Size C (2.75mm) crochet hook

2 small black hooks and eyes

Scissors

SIZES

Small – to fit wrists 6 in (15cm)– 6¾ in (17cm)

Medium – to fit wrists 6¾ in (17cm)–7½ in (19cm)

Large – to fit wrists 7½ in (19cm)–8¼ in (21cm)

Instructions for the smallest size are given first, larger sizes are in brackets.

Start with the darker shade to give a better look and create a natural border. Alternate by working two rows in each shade. Change yarns during the last stitch in the row before the color change, by working the last loop of the stitch before you need to change yarn using the new yarn so the new color is ready to be used for the turning chain.

special terms

Tr (triple crochet): Wrap the yarn around the hook twice, insert hook into the work, yo, draw a loop through the work, yo, draw through first 2 loops on hook, yo, draw through the next 2 loops on the hook, yo, draw through the last 2 loops on the hook. You will be left with 1 loop on the hook.

PATTERN

Make a slip knot.

Make 44ch.

1st Row (right side) 1sc into 2nd ch from hook, *1sc into next ch, (1hdc into next ch) twice, (1dc into next ch) twice, (1tr into next ch) 3 times, (1dc into next ch) twice, (1hdc into next ch) twice, (1sc into next ch) twice; rep from * to end, turn.

2nd Row 1ch, 1sc into each st to end, turn.

Change to other color yarn.

3rd Row 4ch (count as 1tr), skip first st, *1tr into next st, (1dc into next st) twice, (1hdc into next st) twice, (1sc into next st) 3 times, (1hdc into next st) twice, (1dc into next st) twice, (1tr into next st) twice; rep from * to end, turn.

4th Row 1ch, 1sc into each st to end, working last sc into top of turning chain, turn.

Change back to first color yarn.

5th Row 1ch, 1sc into first st, *1sc into next st, (1hdc into next st) twice, (1dc into next st) twice, (1tr into

next st) 3 times, (1dc into next st) twice, (1hdc into next st) twice, (1sc into next st) twice; rep from * to end, turn.

6th Row 1ch, 1sc into each st to end, turn.
Repeat 3rd–6th Rows. Don't fasten off.

FINISHING

FOR SMALL SIZE ONLY: 1ch, without turning, work 1 round of sc evenly around three sides of the cuff, working 3sc into each corner.

MEDIUM AND LARGE SIZES: Work a round of sc around three sides of the cuff, working extra rows of sc at row-end edge as follows:
**1st Row 1ch, 1sc into each row end, turn.
2nd Row 1ch, 1sc into each sc to end, turn.

MEDIUM ONLY:
3rd Row 1ch, 1sc into each sc to last sc, 3sc in last sc, don't turn.

LARGE ONLY: Repeat 2nd Row twice more.
Next Row 1ch, 1sc into each sc to last sc, 3sc in last sc, don't turn. **

MEDIUM AND LARGE: Continue to work around the cuff, working 1sc into the back of each ch until you reach the last ch, 3sc in last ch.

Repeat from ** to ** once more.

ALL SIZES: Fasten off, sew in all the ends. Now attach two hooks evenly at one end of the cuff and attach two eyes in corresponding positions at the other end.

> **tip**
> Remember to insert the hook under both strands of the base chain when working a stitch. This will create a firm and even edge.

ZIGZAG CUFF

MATERIALS
1 x 1 ounce (25g) ball Twilleys Goldfingering – light grey, shade 57
1 x 1 ounce (25g) ball Twilleys Goldfingering – purple, shade 60

EQUIPMENT
Size C (2.75mm) crochet hook
2 small black hooks and eyes
Scissors

SIZES
Small – to fit wrists 6in (15cm)– 6¾in (17cm)
Medium – to fit wrists 6¾in (17cm)–7½in (19cm)
Large – to fit wrists 7½in (19in)–8¼in (21cm)

Instructions for the smallest size are given first, larger sizes are in brackets.

Alternate colors by working two rows in each shade. For tips on changing yarn, see wave cuff.

PATTERN
Make a slip knot.
Make 57ch.
1st Row 2sc into 2nd ch from hook, *1sc into each of next 4ch, skip 2ch, 1sc into each of next 4ch, 3sc into next ch; rep from * ending last rep with just 2sc in the last ch, turn.
2nd Row 1ch, 2sc into first st, *1sc into each of next 4 sts, skip 2 sts, 1sc into each of next 4 sts, 3sc into next st; rep from * ending last rep with just 2sc in the last st, turn.
Change to other color yarn.
Repeat 2nd Row 8 times more, working 2 rows using each color.

FINISHING
Finish as for wave cuff.

pretty in pink

You shall go to the ball! A gorgeous choker with rows of pink beads, and threaded through with satin ribbons that tie at the back.

SKILL Intermediate

MATERIALS

1 x ¼ ounce (10g) ball of DMC Coton Perlé 5, shade 761

63in (160cm) of ¼in (6mm) pink satin ribbon

1 tube of Gutermann satin Rocaille 9, shade 4395

EQUIPMENT

Size B (2.25mm) crochet hook

Blunt-ended needle

Collapsible eye beading needle

SIZE

Small – to fit neck size 12in (30cm)–13¾in (35cm)

Medium/large – to fit neck size 14in (36cm)–16 in (40cm)

Instructions for the smaller size are given first; the larger size is in brackets.

Thread 210 (222) beads.

PATTERN

Make 73 (77) ch.

1st Row work 1sc into 2nd ch from hook, 1sc into each ch to end, turn. 72 (76) sts

2nd Row 1ch, 1sc into first st, 1scb into each sc to last sc, 1sc into last sc, turn.

3rd Row 1ch, 1sc into each st to end, turn.

4th Row 3ch, skip first sc, 1dc into each of next 5sc, *1ch, skip 1sc, 1dc into next sc; rep from * to last 6 sts, 1dc into each of next 6sc, turn.

special terms

Tr (triple crochet): Wrap the yarn around the hook twice, insert hook into the work, yo, draw a loop through the work, yo, draw through first 2 loops on hook, yo, draw through the next 2 loops on the hook, yo, draw through the last 2 loops on the hook. You will be left with 1 loop on the hook.

Scb This is one single crochet with a bead. To work a bead into the fabric, slide the bead up the yarn so it is close to the work, insert the hook into the next st, yo, draw through a loop, yo, draw through 2 loops [see above].

5th Row 1ch, 1sc into each dc and each ch sp to end, working last sc into top of tch, turn.
Repeat 2nd–5th Rows once more.
Repeat 2nd and 3rd Rows once more. Fasten off.

FINISHING

Cut the ribbon in half and thread each half onto a needle. Starting with the ribbon at the back, weave in and out of the spaces. Place a small dab of glue or nail polish on the ends of the ribbon so that it doesn't fray.

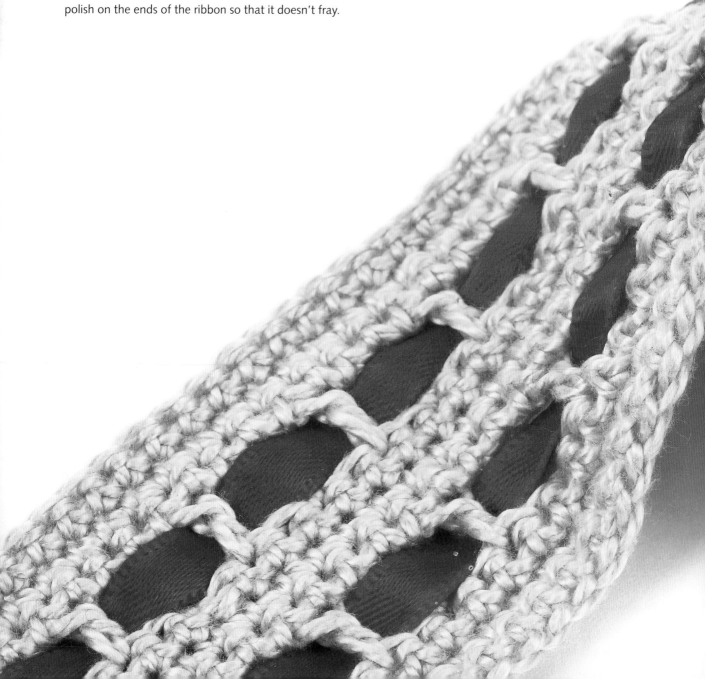

flower hair clips

You can make lots of these pretty hair clips in different color combinations – they are so quick and easy.

SKILL Easy

MATERIALS

DMC Coton Perlé 5 point, shades 211, 962, 3326, and 899

Bobby pins

Strong craft glue

Large star sequins (1 per slide)

EQUIPMENT

Size A (2mm) crochet hook

Needle

Scissors

PATTERN

Using color A (any color), make 5ch, join in a ring with a sl st.

1st Round 1ch, work 10sc into ring, sl st into first sc.

2nd Round 1ch, 2sc into each sc, sl st into first sc. (20 sts)

3rd Round 2ch, working into the front loop only *1dc into each of next 3sc, 2ch, sl st into next st; rep from * 4 more times working last sl st into base of first 2ch. (5 petals made.) Fasten off.

Working into the back loop only, attach color B (any color, not A) into the back loop of first sc, *3ch, 2tr into each of next 3sc, 3ch, sl st into next sc; rep from * 4 more times, working last sl st into base of first 3ch. Fasten off.

special terms

flo (front loop only): Work the stitch in the normal way, but inserting the hook under the front loop only of each st.

blo (back loop only): Work the stitch in the normal way, but inserting the hook under the back loop only of each st [see above].

tr (triple crochet): Wrap the yarn around the hook twice, insert hook into the work, yo, draw a loop through the work, yo, draw through first 2 loops on the hook, yo, draw through the next 2 loops on the hook, yo, draw through the last 2 loops on the hook. You will be left with 1 loop on the hook.

FINISHING

Sew in all the ends and press the flower flat. Now slide onto a bobby pin. Attach the sequin to the center of the flower with a small dab of glue.

berry bead earrings

Pretty pendant earrings worked in a swirl of berry colored beads. They are made using only the most basic techniques and are an easy project for a beginner to try.

SKILL Easy

MATERIALS
1 tube of Gutermann Rocaille 9 seed beads, shade 5435
1 x reel of 32 gauge silver jewelry wire
1 pair of earring hooks

EQUIPMENT
Size A (2mm) crochet hook
Flat-nose pliers
Scissors

special terms
Scb: This is one single crochet with a bead. To work a bead into the fabric, slide the bead up the wire so it is close to the fabric, insert hook to the left of the bead and into next stitch, yo, draw through a loop, yo, draw through 2 loops. The bead will now be caught in the stitch.

PATTERN
Thread on 48 beads for each earring.
Make a slip knot.
Make 2ch.
1st Round work 8scb into 2nd ch from hook.
2nd Round 2scb into each st. (16 sts)
3rd Round * 1scb into next st, 2scb into next st; rep from * to end, sl st into first scb. (24 sts) Fasten off leaving a 4in (10cm) tail.

FINISHING
Thread 15 beads onto the tail, thread the tail through the ring on the bottom of the earring hook, wrap the wire back round itself to secure, and pass through the next couple of beads. Cut the wire close to the beads.

tip
When finishing this off, take care not to overstress the wire, as you may cause it to break.

daisy chain necklace

Delicate white and yellow daisies that can be worked up very quickly
are linked with jump rings and finished with a clasp for a new crocheted
take on a traditional theme.

SKILL Easy

MATERIALS

10 (11) round silver jump rings

1 barrel clasp

1 skein of DMC Mouliné 25, shade 445

1 reel of DMC Coton Perlé 5 point, in white

EQUIPMENT

Size D (2.75mm) crochet hook

Blunt-ended needle

Flat-nosed pliers

Scissors

GAUGE

Each flower should measure 1¼in (3.5cm) from tip to tip.
The flowers do not need to be exactly this size, but you
should ensure they are all the same size to achieve a
uniform look.

SIZE

Small – to fit neck size 12in (30cm)–13¾in (35cm)

Medium/large – to fit neck size 14in (36cm)–16 in (40cm)

PATTERN

Make 11 (12) flowers.

Using the yellow yarn, make a slip knot.

Make 2ch.

1st Round work 5sc into 2nd ch from hook.

2nd Round 2sc into each sc to end. (10 sts)

special terms

Tr (triple crochet): Wrap the yarn round the hook
twice [see above], insert hook into the work, yo,
draw a loop through the work, yo, draw through
first 2 loops on hook, yo, draw through the next 2
loops on the hook, yo, draw through the last 2
loops on the hook. You will be left with 1 loop on
the hook.

3rd Round Using the white yarn,*1sc into next st, 2sc
into next st; rep from* to end. (15 sts)

4th Round *2ch, 1dc into first sc, 1tr into next sc, 1dc
into next sc, 2ch, sl st into next sc; rep from * 4 more
times, working sl st at end of last rep into base of 2ch
at beg of round. Fasten off.

FINISHING

Sew in all the ends. Press the flowers so they are flat.
Now, using a pair of flat-nosed pliers, open a jump
ring and thread it through the top of the tr on any
petal of two flowers. Close the ring. Continue.

tip

When changing color, introduce the new color
into the last loop of the stitch before the actual
color change.

silver chain anklet

A sexy summer ankle chain in a sparkly silver yarn with drop beads and fastened with a barrel clasp. This is very quick to make and uses only a tiny amount of yarn and beads.

SKILL Easy

MATERIALS
1 x 1 ounce (25g) ball Twilleys Goldfingering – silver, shade 5
7 (small) or 8 (medium (large) wire-wrapped beads
1 barrel clasp

EQUIPMENT
Round-nosed pliers
Size B (2.25mm) crochet hook
Collapsible eye beading needle
Blunt-ended needle
Scissors

SIZE
Small – 7½in (19cm); Medium/large – 8½in (22cm)
Instructions for the smaller size are first, instructions for medium/large are in brackets.

special terms
Picot: Make 3ch, sl st into 3rd ch from hook.

PREPARATION – MAKING PENDANT BEADS
So that the beads hang nicely from the chain, instead of threading them directly onto the yarn, they will be suspended on a short length of wire.

For each bead, cut a piece of wire approximately 1¼in (3cm) in length (you may need to use a shorter or longer piece of wire depending on the size of your bead). Using a pair of round-nosed pliers, make a small loop at one end; this is to ensure the bead doesn't slip off. Thread the bead onto the wire and, at the other end, make a slightly larger loop for the yarn to pass through and poke the end of the wire back through the bead.

If you prefer, you can buy beads that already come in a wire cage with a loop for threading.

Thread on 7 (8) beads.

PATTERN

Make a slip knot.

Make 45 (51) ch.

1st Row Work 1sc into 2nd ch from hook, 1sc into each ch to end, turn. 44 (50) sts

2nd Row 5ch, skip first 3sc, 1sc into next sc, work 1 picot, 1sc into next sc, *5ch, skip 4sc, 1sc into next sc, work 1 picot, 1sc into next sc; rep from * to last 3sc, 2ch, skip 2 sc, 1dc into last sc, turn.

3rd Row 1ch, 1sc into first dc, *8ch, 1sc into next 5ch arch; rep from * to end working last sc into 3rd of 5ch, turn.

4th Row 1ch, 1sc into first sc, *(5sc, slide a bead up, 5sc) into next 8ch arch, 1sc into next sc; rep from * to end. Fasten off.

FINISHING

Press the anklet, carefully avoiding the beads. Sew in all the ends. Attach a barrel clasp to each end of the 1st Row.

dangly squares earrings

These pretty earrings are created by making three small wire mesh squares for each earring with delicate pink seed beads worked in. The squares are then linked together with linking rings so that they hang.

SKILL Intermediate

MATERIALS

1 tube of Gutermann Rocaille 9 seed beads, shade 4965

1 reel of 32 gauge silver jewelry wire

1 pair of earring hooks

6 round silver jump rings

Strong craft glue

EQUIPMENT

Flat-nosed pliers

Size A (2mm) crochet hook

Scissors

special terms

Scb: This is one single crochet with a bead. To work a bead into the fabric, slide the bead up the wire so it is close to the fabric, insert hook to the left of the bead and into next stitch, yo, draw through a loop, yo, draw through 2 loops. The bead will now be caught in the stitch.

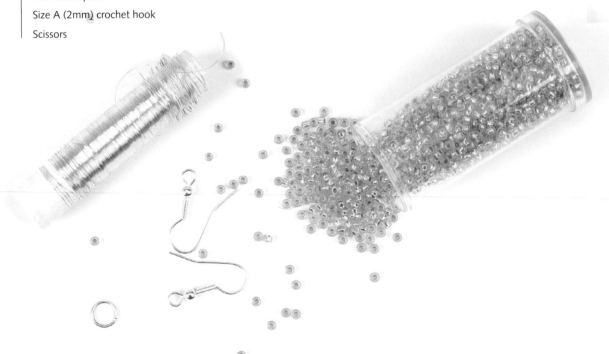

PREPARATION

First, thread on 48 beads for each earring. These are all the beads you will need for each earring, though it may be worth adding a few more just in case you have miscounted.

PATTERN

Make a slip knot.

Make 5ch.

1st Row 1scb into 2nd ch from hook, 1scb into each ch to end, turn. (4 sts)

2nd Row 1ch, 1scb into each scb to end, turn.

3rd and 4th Rows as 2nd row. Fasten off.

Make another 5 mesh squares in this way.

FINISHING

To make up each earring: Weave the wire ends into the mesh and cut. Attach each of the squares with a centrally placed jump ring. You may need to use the pliers to open and close the rings. Now, add a ring to the top center of the top square and attach the earring hook.

tip

As the wire is very fine, and may easily work its way through the gap in the jump rings, seal the rings with a dab of glue applied with a pin.

furry scrunchies

These scrunchies are so easy and super speedy to make and look great in this funky fake fur yarn. One ball will makes lots of scrunchies, so go wild!

SKILL Very easy

MATERIALS
1 x 2 ounce (50g) ball of Patons Whisper in shades bloom, gem, and jet
1 hair band for each scrunchy

EQUIPMENT
Size G (4mm) crochet hook
Blunt-ended needle
Scissors

PATTERN
Hold the hair band in front of the yarn, between the thumb and middle finger of your left hand. Insert the hook into the middle of the band, wrap the yarn around the hook, draw the hook back through the band, wrap the yarn around the hook, and draw through the loop on the hook.

Insert the hook into the band again, yo, draw the hook through the band, yo, draw the hook through both loops on the hook; this will leave 1 loop. This makes 1 single crochet.

4ch (count as 1dc and 1ch), *1dc, 1ch; rep from * all the way around the band until it is no longer visible even when stretched out. Sl st into top of 4ch. Cut the end and draw the tail through the final loop. Sew in both ends.

two-tone ring bangles

This project is one of the quickest in the book. Taking only minutes to make, this elegant and chic looking bracelet in two tones of yarn is worked in single crochet around a series of small rings.

SKILL Easy

MATERIALS
6 or 7 x 1in (25mm) brass rings (curtain accessories)
1 skein of Anchor Mouliné, shades 102 and 108

EQUIPMENT
Size B (2.25mm) crochet hook
Blunt-ended needle
Scissors

SIZE
Small – to fit wrists 6in (15cm)–7in (18cm), use 6 rings
Medium/large – to fit 7in (18cm)–8¼in (21cm), use 7 rings

GAUGE
Although gauge is not important for this pattern, the stitches should be fairly tight and fit snugly around the ring.

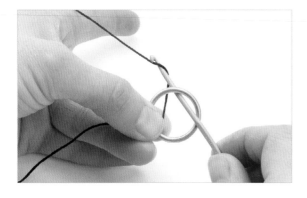

PATTERN
Using shade 108, hold the yarn in your left hand in the normal way, and you will also need to hold the first ring between the thumb and middle finger of your left hand. Insert the hook into the ring from front to back, wrap the yarn around the hook, draw the loop back through the ring, wrap the yarn around the hook, and draw through the loop on the hook [see bottom left].

Insert the hook into the ring, yo, draw loop back through the ring, yo, draw hook through both loops on the hook, this will leave 1 loop. This makes 1 single crochet.

Work a further 15sc into the center of the ring. Now add a new ring. Holding the new ring in your left hand between your thumb and middle finger, insert the hook into this new ring, yo, draw the loop back through the ring, yo, draw through both loops on the hook. This is 1sc.

Work a further 15sc into the 2nd ring.

Continue in this way, working 16sc around each new ring. On the final ring, change yarn after the first 16sc and, using shade 102, work a further 16sc, ending with a sl st into the first sc on that ring.

Now sl st into final sc on the previous ring, and work 16sc around that ring, ending with a sl st into the first sc on that ring.

Cont to work 16 more sc around each ring, ending with a sl st into the first sc of each ring until you are back at the first ring, ending with a sl st into the first sc on that ring. Join the bracelet into a ring by working a sl st into stitches 16 and 17 on the final ring. Fasten off. Sew in all the ends.

Make a bigger impact by using two really contrasting colors, rather than two shades of the same one. Try black and white, as shown here, for example.

floribunda barrette

A cornucopia of brightly colored flowers on a leafy background makes a striking hair accessory that is very simple and quick to make.

SKILL Easy

MATERIALS

1 skein each of DMC Mouliné 25 thread, shades 608, 603, 321, and 909
1 plain barrette approximately 2¾in (7cm) in length
Strong craft glue

EQUIPMENT

Size B (2.75mm) crochet hook
Blunt-ended tapestry needle
Scissors

FLOWERS

These flowers are worked in a spiral and it takes only a few minutes to make each one. Using shades 608, 603, and 321, make 7 flowers.

Make a slip knot.
Make 2ch.
1st Round work 8sc into 2nd ch from hook.
2nd Round 2dc into each sc to end. (16 sts)
3rd Round Skip first 2dc, 1sc around stem of next 8dc, 1sc around stem of each of next 2sc in row below, sl st around stem of next sc. Fasten off.

LEAFY BACKGROUND

If your barrette is a different size to the one suggested in this pattern, you may need any multiple of four more or fewer chain stitches to start with, bearing in mind the base will stretch up to ⅜in (1cm) in length.

Make a slip knot.
Using DMC shade 909, make 15ch.
1st Round work 1sc into 2nd ch from hook, 1sc into each ch to last ch, work 3sc into last ch. Now working into the back of the base ch, work 1sc into each ch to end, work 2sc into first ch of 2ch, sl st into 2nd ch of 2ch. (32 sts)
2nd Round 2ch, 3dc into first sc, 3tr into next st, 3dc into next st, (1hdc, 1sc) into next st, *3dc into next st, 3tr into next st, 3dc into next st, (1hdc, 1sc) into next st; rep from * to end, sl st into top of 2ch. Fasten off.

FINISHING

Using a crochet hook, draw the tails of the flowers through the leafy background from front to back, and tie the tails in a knot to secure the flowers. Sew in the ends. Remember, you will not see the back of the leafy background. Now glue the background to the barrette.

boho beads

Boho beads are crocheted balls. For a great bohemian look, string the balls to make a necklace or bracelet. You can even mix with them with glass beads. Make it short or long, multicolored – whatever you like!

SKILL Easy

NECKLACE – LARGE BEADS

MATERIALS
1 x 2 ounce (50g) ball of Rowan Cotton Glace in Excite
1 tube of Gutermann ⅓in (8mm) glass beads, shade 1000
Small bag of polyester filling or cotton wool
1 barrel clasp
2 crimps

EQUIPMENT
Flat-nosed pliers
Size E (3.5mm) crochet hook
Blunt-ended needle
Scissors

GAUGE
Each ball should measure 1in (3cm) in diameter or at least be of a uniform size.

PATTERN
For a short necklace interspersed with beads and finished with a clasp, make 12 balls. For a longer necklace that fits over the head, make at least 24 balls.
Make a slip knot.
Make 2ch.
1st Round work 8sc into 2nd ch from hook.
2nd Round 2sc into each sc to end. (16 sts)
3rd Round *1sc into each of the next 3sc, 2sc into next sc; rep from * to end. (20 sts)
4th Round 1sc into each sc to end.
5th Round *1sc into each of next 3sc, sc2tog into next sc; rep from * to end. (16 sts)
Place filling into the ball.
6th Round sc2tog 8 times. (8 sts)
7th Round 1sc into each sc to end.
Fasten off. Sew in the ends.

FINISHING
Using a sharp needle, thread the crocheted balls, alternating with glass beads if you like. Now, at each end, thread on a crimp and then the clasp, and take the thread back through the crimp. Using the pliers, crush the crimp flat. This will hold the clasp in place. Trim off any excess thread.

If you are making your necklace long enough to fit over your head, you may decide not to have a clasp. In that case, simply thread the beads onto a piece of sturdy cotton thread and tie the ends firmly. Conceal the ends within the balls.

> **tip**
> These balls are a good way of using up odds and ends of yarn, though different yarns may make different-sized balls.

BRACELET – SMALL BEADS

MATERIALS

1 x 2 ounce (50g) ball of Rowan Cotton Glace in Tickle

Small bag of polyester filling or cotton wool

Shirring elastic

EQUIPMENT

Size E (3.5mm) crochet hook

Blunt-ended needle

Scissors

GAUGE

Each ball should measure 1 in (2.5cm) in diameter using a Size E (3.5mm) hook. Although it doesn't matter what size your beads are, you should ensure they are all the same size for a neat and uniform look.

SIZES

Small – to fit wrists 6in (15cm)–6¾in (17cm)

Medium – to fit wrists 6¾in (17cm)–7½in (19cm)

Large – to fit wrists 7½in (19cm)–8¼in (21cm)

Instructions for the smallest size are given first, larger sizes are in brackets.

PATTERN

Make 11 (13, 15) balls.

Make a slip knot.

Make 2ch.

1st Round work 8sc into 2nd ch from hook.

2nd Round 2sc into each sc to end. (16 sts)

3rd and 4th Rounds 1sc into each sc to end.

Place filling into the ball.

5th Round sc2tog 8 times. (8 sts)

6th Round 1sc into each sc to end.

Fasten off. Sew in the ends.

Now, using a sharp needle, thread the beads onto the elastic. Cut the elastic and tie a knot. Sew in the ends.

Resources

Or substitute a fun fur such as Berroco Crystal FX, Berroco Hush, or Berroco Lavish, all available at:
www.woolneedlework.com
www.yarnia.com
www.yarns-and.com

Crystal Palace BeBop available at:
www.yarnmarket.com

Lion Brand Fancy Fur available at:
www.joann.com

Lion Brand Festive Fur available at:
www.discountyarnsale.com
www.hancockfabricstore.com
www.joann.com

Tumbling Tendrils Earrings
Ribbon Hairband
Tubular Jewelry
Anchor Arista can be substituted with Lurex yarns such as Katia's Gatsby, GGH's Lame, Crystal Palace's Deco Stardust, Takhi Star, or Rowan Lurex Shimmer, all available at: www.yarnmarket.com

Other Great Yarns that Can Be
  Used in These Projects:
Anny Blatt Gyps d'Anny (metallic,
  4 sts/in)
Cascade Di.Ve Luxus and
  Di.Ve Nostro Oro are thicker
  metallic tapes
Karabella Diamonds (viscose/poly,
  3.5 sts/in)
Karabella Gossamer
  (mohair/nylon/poly, 5 sts/in)
Karabella Glimmer (rayon/Lurex,
  5.5 sts/in)

INTERNET RESOURCES FOR BEADS AND JEWELRY-MAKING SUPPLIES

www.arizonabeadcompany.com
www.artbeads.com
www.astralbeads.com
www.beaddiner.com
www.beadshop.com
www.beadstudio.com
www.craftland.net

www.eebeads.com
www.findingking.com
www.firemountaingems.com
www.gypsywindbeads.com
www.jansjewels.com
www.jewelrysupply.com
www.jewelrytelevision.com
www.johnnasgifts.com
www.landofodds.com
www.ninadesigns.com
www.orientaltrading.com
www.parawire.com
www.riogrande.com
www.save-on-crafts.com
www.suncountrygems.com
www.wigjig.com
www.wire-sculpture.com

YARN DISTRIBUTORS

Anny Blatt
7796 Boardwalk
Brighton, MI 48116
(800) 531-9276
www.annyblatt.com

Berroco, Inc.
14 Elmdale Road
P.O. Box 367
Uxbridge, MA 01569
(508)278-2527
www.berroco.com

Cascade Yarns, Inc.
1224 Andover Park, E.
Tukwila, WA 98188-3905
(800)548-1048
www.cascadeyarns.com

Coats & Clark
8 Shelter Drive
Greer, SC 29650
(864) 877-8985
www.coatsandclark.com

Colinette
28 N. Bacton Road
Malvern, PA 19355
(610) 644-4885
www.colinette.com

Crystal Palace Yarns
160 23rd Street

Richmond, CA 94804
(800) 666-7455
www.straw.com

DMC Corp
#10F Port Kearny
South Hackensack Avenue
South Kearny, NJ 07032
(973) 589-0606
www.dmc-usa.com

Habu Textiles
135 West 29th Street, Suite 804
New York, NY 10001
(212) 239-3546
www.habutextiles.com

Karabella Yarn
1201 Broadway
New York, NY 10001
(212) 684-2665
www.karabellayarns.com

Lion Brand Yarn Co.
34 West 15th Street
New York, NY 10011
(212) 243-8995
www.lionbrand.com

Muench/GGH
1323 Scott Street
Petaluma, CA 94954
(800) 733-9276
www.meunchyarns.com

Patons
2700 Dufferin Street
Unit 1, Toronto, ONT M6B 4J3
Canada

Tahki/Stacey Charles
70-30 80th Street
Building #36
Ridgewood, NY 11385
(718) 326-4433
www.takhistacycharles.com

Westminster Fibers (Rowan, Nashua, etc.)
4 Townsend West, Unit 8
Nashua, NH 03063
(800)445-9276
www.knitrowan.com

index

Page numbers in *italics* refer to picture captions and boxes